Identifying Shrubs—Made Easy

- **Identification** section (pages 60 to 207)

Color photos of wild and ornamental shrubs, with information on their characteristics, leaves, flowers, fruits, and bark; plant profiles with descriptions of all the major distinguishing features and of similar species.

- **Barron's color key**
(see inside the front foldout, opposite)
Colored bars and leaf symbols guide you to the four groups of shrubs:
  - Yellow: Shrubs with single, smooth-margined leaves
  - Green: Shrubs with dentate, serrate, crenate, or lobed leaves
  - Blue: Shrubs with compoun (pinnate) leaves
  - Lilac: Shrubs with needle-lik scale-like leaves

- **"Shrubs with E.. le Fruits"**
(see back fold'ou
A selected group of w d nd
ornamental shrubs wit.   uits

← **Please** ⟵

Mountain Cranberry in fruit (Vaccinium vitis-idaea);
from Lukmanier Pass in the Swiss Alps

Information and Warnings

● Many of the berries or berry-like fruits produced
by ornamental and wild shrubs are inedible or range
from mildly to lethally poisonous.

● Pay close attention to the sections of the
profiles that tell whether a fruit is edible, inedible,
or poisonous!

● For accurate identification, you need to make
exact comparisons between each one of the distinguishing features described here, along with the
accompanying photo, and the plant you have
found. If even one of the features is not a match,
you have to assume that what you have found is
not the fruit described in this book!

● If you plan to eat what you gather, pick only
fruits that you know well!

Barron's
Nature Guide

SHRUBS

in the Wild and in Gardens

Bruno P. Kremer

Consulting Editor:
Dennis W. Stevenson, Ph.D.
Administrator, Harding Laboratory
The New York Botanical Garden

Important wild shrubs and
ornamental woody plants

Identifying, Learning about,
and Planting

Special guide section:
Shrubs in the garden

500 color photos by
well-known photographers

BARRON'S 30 drawings by Marlene Gemke

Contents

Crowberries covered with hoarfrost

Preface

Identifying Shrubs

Planting Shrubs

Shrubs fashion the image of our landscape just as much as trees do. In spring they are studded with white, yellow, or red flowers. In summer they form green borders along the edges of woods, paths, and streets. In fall they either are resplendent in their bright foliage or bear brilliantly colored fruits. Over and above that, they provide a habitat, a shelter, and food for a great many kinds of animals.

This new Barron's nature guide to shrubs presents the most common wild shrubs, as well as a large number of ornamental shrubs for garden use. Splendid color photos show the external appearance, leaf shapes, flowers, and fruits, along with details such as buds, bark, spines, and prickles. In the profiles, the appearance, blooming season, occurrence, and characteristic features are described. Similar species also are briefly described. In addition, you will learn what the site requirements of each particular species are and what value the species has for native wildlife. The reliable Barron's color key makes identification easy, even for those with little experience in the field of botany. To help you locate the shrubs quickly, we have arranged them in four groups, based on their leaf shapes.

This new Barron's guide is more than a book for identification of shrubs. In the chapters "Learning about Shrubs" and "Experiencing Shrubs," the author presents the various growth forms of shrubs, describes their changing appearance throughout the four seasons, and points out their significance as a habitat for animals.

The chapter "Planting Shrubs" deals with the planting of wild and ornamental shrubs in the countryside and in gardens.

The author and the editors of Barron's series of nature books wish you a great deal of pleasure as you identify and plant wild and ornamental shrubs.

Sloes are the first to dress up the countryside with their blossoms.

Learning about Shrubs

Almost everywhere, we share our habitat with plants. However, many of them are so tiny that we either overlook them altogether or take little notice of them—the coating of algae on an old wall, the cushions of moss in pavement cracks, the grasses and weeds between the asphalt and concrete. Shrubs and trees, on the other hand, readily catch our eye. In settled areas, they line roads and paths; in gardens and parks, they form vital islands of greenery. Moreover, wherever land is cultivated by man, they provide decorative backdrops and serve to organize the rural landscape. Their distinctive feature is the lignification—or conversion to wood—of virtually all the tissues in the root and shoot axis systems. For this reason, shrubs and trees are known as woody or timber plants.

What Is a Shrub?

At one extreme, woody plants include trees that grow barely as tall as a match; at the other extreme, this category also includes shrubs that truly put a tree in the shade.

What Is a Tree?
By a tree, we mean a woody plant that is clearly subdivided into an upright, well-developed main trunk and a crown, or top, with a great many branches. Although free-standing trees may be covered with branches growing very low on

Transitional Solutions
A distinction has to be made between the so-called subshrubs—plants in which gradual transitions to herbs or herbaceous plants are evident—and the true shrubs, all of whose supporting parts become completely woody. With subshrubs, only the base of the small trunk and the main branches become woody to the core. The younger branches or twigs, by comparison, stay green, soft, and herbaceous for quite some time. Unlike the herbs and herbaceous plants, they survive the fall

In the photo: A well-developed single trunk and a wide-spreading treetop, silhouetted here—a tree fit for a picture book. This hedgerow thorn has succeeded in becoming a splendid free-standing specimen, all alone in a broad meadow with no competitors.

the trunk and hence have a bushy look, in most cases the lower portion of the trunk is free of branches. Only higher up does the load-bearing column of the trunk divide into several large, ascending main branches.

What Is a Shrub?
Shrubs lack the clear, towering main trunk. Their shoot axis branches just above the ground into several main stems of roughly the same stoutness and, barely a foot above the ground, assumes dense, bushy, and impenetrable configurations. For this reason, a shrub could be described as a treetop located directly above the ground. The branching pattern and the position of the branches of shrubs and treetops are generally quite similar. A few species deviate from that scheme however.

and winter months, lengthen by means of apical growth when the vegetative season starts again, and generally become woody only in the second or third year. Many time-honored scented and aromatic plants such as sage or thyme are neither herbs nor true shrubs, but subshrubs.

Quite a number of woody species can develop into either shrubby or treelike shapes. An example is European elder, which usually occurs as a bush, but can be a tree, particularly when free-standing. The same is true of holly, which can attain a considerable height.

Under special growing conditions, even very well-defined species of woody plants are subject to a striking change in shape. For example, near the climatic tree line in the high mountains, the red beech, which usually manages to attain impos-

Tree or shrub?

Witch hazel adorned with blossoms in winter

ing tree shapes, becomes a broad bush with stems that rest on the ground. A plant's common name is not always a reliable indication of the ultimate shape. For example, the spindle tree is not a tree at all, but a medium- to large-sized shrub. While actually only a few species of woody plants can become either shrubby or arborescent based on the site or habitat conditions, nature does not permit the alternation of form between subshrub and shrub or tree. Similarly, "subtrees" are also unknown. Naturally, the density of a shrub's branches has a major effect on its outward appearance. Some species develop only a few main stems, while others construct virtually impenetrable

In the photo: Despite its respectable mature height, witch hazel is really a shrub. It clearly has a multitude of small trunks, and its crown begins near ground level.

thickets. Moreover, shrubs can grow in unbroken, slender, almost columnar shapes, or in outstretched, broad ones. Their overall appearance depends on which stems are more strongly developed, the lower ones (as in the case of juniper) or the upper ones (as in the case of elder).

Growth Forms—a Theme with Variations

Frequently, the woody plants' way of life and their growth form each give rise to the other. Because the shrubby woody plants in the natural landscape also take part in extremely diverse types of biological communities, they frequently have been subjected to the pressure of special ecological conditions. Any plant that wishes to conquer and make use of extraordinary sites also has to make appropriate adaptations in terms of shape and physiological performance. The following types of shrub flora provide some quite impressive examples.

Evergreens

For example, there are the sclerophyllous shrubs, whose perennial evergreen leaves have a coarse, leathery feel, while the leaves of the deciduous broad-leaved woody plants remain fairly thin-skinned and soft. Among the sclerophyllous species, the outer integument (epidermis) is specially supported by deliberate thickenings of the cell wall. Wax impregnation of the surface provides additional waterproofing and thus guarantees even better protection against transpiration. The

species in question, therefore, are extremely well prepared for prolonged summer drought.

Evergreen, coarse-leaved species like box or holly appreciate the dry, warm regions, but their ranges also extend far into the mild-winter regions. Bay laurel, on the other hand, is a genuine inhabitant of southern Europe; in northern and cooler regions it requires special winter protection, and it can be overwintered outdoors only in unusual instances.

All these sclerophyllous species are comparatively unaffected by irregular watering, because their excellent transpiration shield enables them to be quite economical with the precious liquid.

Shrubs with Wandlike Stems

Shrubs with wandlike stems display an equally impressive adaptation to an unreliable or very limited water supply. Their leaves, which usually have a fairly small surface, can be shed quite prematurely for reasons of water economy. In these particular shrubby woody plants, the life-preserving task of sunlight-powered formation of organic compounds, or photosynthesis, falls primarily to the slender green stems and branches. Such adaptations are shown, for example, by Scotch broom with its slender, dark green branches, large portions of whose length are leafless. Scotch broom can colonize

In the photo: Gorse species dispense with flat leaves altogether. The vital substances the plants need are produced in the green tissues of the sharp spines.

Dwarfs and giants

Bluntleaf willow in the flowering stage

very dry, stony soils far more success-fully than shrub species with the broad-leaved foliage. The small winged broom, which thrives in sandy fields and dry grassy areas, also belongs to this species. Spanish broom and gorse also shift the major portion of their metabolic processes into the stems and branches. Butcher's broom exhibits a unique feature. In this plant, the branches broaden out like leaves in order to have a larger surface area to receive the energy-supplying rays of the sun.

Low-spreading Shrubs
Usually we think of shrubs as woody plants of respectable size, at least as tall as a man. However, in special locations, shrubs deviate considerably from this image. Above the timberline in the high mountains, unusually small willow species occur, such as netvein dwarf wil-

In the photo: Low-spreading shrubs like the Alpine dwarf willows with their matchstick format are among the smallest woody plants of all.

low and wideleaf dwarf willow. Often all one can see of these woody plants is the terminal portions of the tiny trunks or stems that protrude from the ground and are roughly the length of a match. The greater part of the plant grows creeping underground. These plants are known as low-spreading shrubs. They nestle closely together in dense matlike or car-petlike stands, thus avoiding the onslaught of the wind, and in the cold season they can use the blanket of snow as protection against freezing. One is almost tempted to describe these woody

Alpine bearberry in its fall aspect

"half-pints" as natural bonsais. However, while the artistically designed dwarf trees from the Far East are produced by tending, pruning, and wiring them into the proper shape, the form of the Arctic or Alpine low-spreading shrubs is largely determined by their genetic constitution; it represents a response to the very brief periods of productivity and/or growth in their cold, snowy habitats.

Dwarf Shrubs

While low-spreading shrubs are natural ground covers, and rise to a height of scarcely more than a fingerlength, the dwarf shrub category is the next step up in terms of size. This group includes, for example, black crowberry, mountain cranberry, blueberry, heather, and dwarf birch. Somewhere between a hand's length and knee-high, they also produce thick-growing, extremely small bushes

In the photo: Only deciduous broad-leaved shrubs put on such a magical show of colors in fall.

that brave the wind and weather. They are characterized by their optimal use of the heat in the ground and also—owing to their small leaves—by their highly efficient protection against transpiration. They also can overcome site problems that would be the complete undoing of other deciduous shrubs. It is no accident that extensive, far-flung tracts of heathland covered with dwarf shrubs are common in the high mountains and the Arctic tundra. The few regions of bog in North America reproduce these special conditions of life only in some sections, but they also sustain a very distinctive vege-

14

Inconceivable beauty

In the photo: Dwarf shrubs—like this mountain cranberry—together with other species such as conifer seedlings and cup lichens create a habitat of small dimensions, whose diversity is usually overlooked.

tation of woody plants, consisting largely of dwarf shrubs.

Prickly and Spiny Shrubs

If you snag your trousers on a blackberry shoot or inadvertently put your hand into some prickly boxwood, it feels pretty unpleasant. Many plants exhibit a downright painful ability to penetrate the skin, making every slight contact and particularly every hearty grip into a disagreeable acupuncture session.

A grave ecological state of affairs is reflected in the impressively tough fortifications of many plants. The statement that there can be no animal or human life without plants sounds plausible and almost self-evident. Less banal and even quite astonishing, however, is the reverse: The higher plants would certainly not exist in the form familiar to us today if they had not found it necessary to defend themselves against animals since primeval times. During many millions of years of evolution, the voracity of animals has made a truly strict selection among plants. The relationship could equally be described as a mutual arms race.

In every natural biological community the green plants have the somewhat thankless task of serving as food for the multitude of animal vegetarians. But over time, the plants have progressed beyond mere passivity. They have developed increasingly ingenious and varied responses to the incursions of planteaters. Many plants defend themselves with poison or a bad taste, with thorns and prickles—they have become armed and hard to grasp from any angle. When shrubs like climbing roses, barberry, and sloe become reinforced fortresses on all fronts, they defend themselves successfully against the large ruminants. However, they are no match for insect larvae, which can get to their green meal in a spiky thicket with no trouble.

We use the term **prickle** whenever the well-fortified barb develops from the surface tissue of the stalk or stem. The gooseberry's German name "prickleberry" is well deserved. Blackberry vines and roses are also prickly shrubs.

On the other hand, **spines** or **thorns** are completely modified leaves (as in the case of barberry) or branches (as in the case of sloe).

Twining and Climbing Shrubs

Sometimes plants achieve several goals at once with their special adaptations. The long, backward-curving prickles on the branches and beneath the leaves of

Ivy (above), clematis (below)

blackberry bushes and rose bushes are not only a splendid preventive means, but also a technically perfect climbing support that works on the principle of the expansion hook and climbing iron. Blackberry thickets and rose hedges are so completely impenetrable precisely because the individual stems and branches also latch onto one another and get their hooks into other surfaces as well.

Besides the climbing plants, other highly unusual woody plants include the twining and vinelike plants, which ascend in the manner of lianas and easily take over brick or stone walls, wire fences, and the topmost regions of other woody plants. This growth type is represented by woodbine honeysuckle. Clematis, which attains great heights, climbs by means of its sturdy petioles, or leafstalks. In many biological communities—for example, bordering the water in lowland woods or on woods edges—it can form very dense curtains many yards high, whose tangle of stems is hardly inferior to the lianas of the tropical rain forests. Twining shrubs always have a fixed direction of convolution. If the stem apex moves in a counterclockwise direction as it grows, the shrub is a left-hand climber. Almost all twining plants follow this pattern. Only the honeysuckle species are right-hand climbers. Among the ornamental woody plants, too, there are some distinctly aggressive upstarts; like the Chinese wisteria, which is a left-hand twining shrub. Ivy, which overwhelms entire walls and climbs up the trunks of trees to weave through the treetops, is a root climber, seeking every-

In the photos: Ivy trunks, as thick as a man's arm, produce fine aerial rootlets wherever they make contact (above). Clematis species (below) climb by means of their leafstalks.

The burden others bear

Boston ivy with red fall foliage

where to establish firm contact with the underlying surface on which it grows. Especially ingenious adhesive disks are displayed by some Virginia creepers, which even conquer totally smooth faces of houses. Despite their considerable mature height, these woody plants produce only a rather slight axial system, because they do not bear their own weight.

Semiparasites
Plants that essentially feed themselves, but in some areas are dependent on supplies of substances forced from or willingly given by a partner, are known as semiparasites.

This category is exemplified by the evergreen mistletoes—spherical, densely branching small woody plants that have lost their roots, settling instead on the boughs of certain species of deciduous or

In the photo: *Parthenocissus* can conquer even very smooth walls. Some forms produce special adhesive disks on the tendrils for that purpose.

coniferous trees and thus entering into special dependent relationships. A normal water supply is not possible on their lofty perch, because mistletoe leaves cannot collect and use water directly. Consequently, these plants have to connect up to an existing and well-functioning water line—their host plant's pathways of conduction. As they grow, mistletoe seedlings use all sorts of tricks in a highly concerted effort to establish direct contact with the water-conducting woody layers of the host. Then they simply tap into these layers. The substances they steal, however, are restricted to the water and the minerals dissolved in it. Organic sub-

Learning about shrubs

In the photo: In old fruit trees, mistletoe—a plant of great ecological interest—often produces an evergreen sheath.

Leaves—acting as flat-spread antennas—are assigned the important task of catching as many light waves as possible from the solar radiation, so that their energy can power the synthesis of substances in the leaf tissues. If only a small amount of dusky light is available, then the efficiency of the antennas can be improved by increasing the pigment content. The deep green coloration of some shrubs of the forest floor, therefore, is a remarkable feat of adaptation to the "dark sides" of their habitat, which in places are quite pronounced.

Characteristically, evergreen broad-leaved shrubs, such as holly or boxwood species, settle in the undergrowth of the forest. Only during the fall and winter weeks, when taller shrubs and trees have shed their leaves and stand bare, do they stand fully in the light, still engaging in photosynthesis.

stances produced by the host plant, such as sugar or amino acids, are not diverted by mistletoe for its own use. It manufactures such substances itself, since it possesses normal green, metabolically active leaves.

Dark Shapes

Even at noon on a bright summer day, deep shadow reigns in a deciduous summer forest, particularly on the floor of an evergreen coniferous forest. Despite extremely unfavorable light conditions, some shrubs like woodbine honeysuckle, blackberry, holly, and in some places boxwood and creeping plants like periwinkle and ivy on the forest floor, grow and thrive even in a dense forest stand.

How are such species able to lead an obviously successful existence in the shade, under these photosynthesis-inhibiting conditions? A more detailed comparison of their foliage with the leaves of shrubs from brighter, more open habitats solves a part of this puzzle, because all the shrub species named above bear extremely dark green, sometimes even black-green, leaves. Evidently the leaf organs contain more chlorophyll per unit of surface area than those of the plants in sunny habitats.

In the photo: A new rose in old surroundings—the climbing rose 'Fugue' was produced by breeders in 1958.

Standing in the shadows

Shrubs in Their Habitat

It is really quite astonishing that the trees indigenous to Central Europe, despite the region's extensive woods and cultivated forests, number fewer than 50 different species. By contrast, there are more than 100 native species of shrubs. Nonetheless, the inventory of native species of woody plants is comparatively modest—a symbol of the consequences of a momentous turning point in the history of that region's flora, a turn of events brought about by the various ice ages.

Blame It on the Ice Age
Relatively few groups of species have survived the deterioration of the climate over the past few thousand years, because the Carpathians, the Alps, and the Pyrenees, which run east to west, prevented them from beating a convenient retreat into alternative quarters located farther south. In North America and East Asia, all the large folded mountain ranges run in a north-south direction. So, species that required warmth could reach more southerly regions with greater ease and thus survive. For Central Europe, then, the ice ages caused an enormous depletion of species, which can even be expressed in concrete numbers through comparison with the floras of other regions. While there are only two *Cornus* species in Central Europe, comparable parts of North America are home to almost 10 times as many species. In Central Europe, forest-forming woody plants are distributed over a scant two dozen different species; by contrast, several hundred woody plant species occur in the same climate region in North America or East Asia.

Woody plants appear greater in visual variety and richer in species than the figures indicate, and this is almost always attributable to shrubs. New growth on the trees and especially the shrubs make the scene appear more vivid and enrich the structure of the woodlands. Were it not for variety created by shrubs, a woods' edge with its multiple gradations would not contrast clearly with adjoining cultivated land. In a forest that is close to the natural state, at least two stories would be missing from the layers of plant heights without shrubs. The two stories include the tier of shrubs close to the ground and the intermediate story, which creates a transition to the upper canopy regions. Without shrubs, the entire agricultural landscape also would be substantially poorer than it already seems after the consolidation and reconfiguration of arable land and the expansion of the scale of production.

Natural Stands
Many shrubs in a landscape are the result of human intervention, but naturally occuring stands do exist. In the various mountain regions of North America, comparatively few of the thickets made up of wild shrubs colonize naturally unwooded sites. Such habitats include the extensive dwarf shrub stands of the high Alpine meadows and tundras which thrive in very shallow soils; and—an oddity deserving special mention—the fringe of small woody plants found at the edges of the tideways in the tideland regions of the North Sea and composed of a single shrub species (knee-high, gray-green sea purslane). In the Central European interior, the shrubby willow thickets in the riparian and delta formation zones of bodies of stagnant water, in lowland bogs and low or marshy meadows, or at the edges of upland bogs also qualify as natural communities of shrubs. This category also includes the various woodland formations on rocky, steep slopes along the valleys of the low mountain ranges. All other occurrences of shrubs, however,

Rich rural landscape

Meadowland shrubs and trees as a landscape backdrop

are elements of the landscape developed and cultivated by man, and as such they are not natural, but at best close to nature.

Shrubs in the Open Fields

Two factors essentially shape the appearance of cultivated land: the natural relief with its mountain chains, valley indentations, and areas of level land, and the cover of vegetation in all its manifestations. The colorful mosaic of wooded regions, meadows and pastures, and croplands permanently define the nature and effect of the lowland regions, the low mountain regions, and a great part of the high mountain landscape. What to an earth-bound observer may look like a lively succession of tracts with various types of use, often appears as a chaotic composition in aerial photographs. Whether such sections of landscape are found particularly beautiful and harmo-

In the photo: Woody species in the open meadows—in the form of single trees or rows of shrubs—are connecting elements. They create linkages between biotopes and maintain relationships between habitats.

nious depends on the structural element. Irrespective of the specific features of the natural relief, the agricultural landscape always is deemed beautiful if the fields and meadows also include a large number of woody plants. Woody plants, in the form of groups of bushes, hedgerows, or groups of single trees, have an unbelievable three-dimensional effect as set pieces or backdrops for country scenery, whether they line paths and roads or trace the plot boundaries between the fields and meadows. Standing alone, arranged in rows, or combined in relatively large

Learning about shrubs

Living and running a farm in a wooded area

groups, shrubs and trees emphasize the special shapes of the terrain features and thus are an unmistakable component of the landscape's character. Particularly in rural settlements, they also form part of the townscape and dovetail effectively with the woody plants of the open fields—tying them together and successfully interlacing them from an ecological point of view as well.

All the thickets and small meadowland stands made up of various shrub species owe their development and character to the humans who use and manage the land; these plants are genuine elements of the cultivated landscape. Hedges in particular, which are unnatural, merit special attention because, in addition to their pleasing visual effect on the aesthetics of the landscape, also are extremely valuable microhabitats. Often they have developed from quickset hedges or other

plantings of shrubs or small trees that served as field boundaries.

Hedges—a Green Ribbon of Sympathy

Hedges are shrubby woody plants arranged in lines or belts. These plants usually do not reach their full mature height and, unlike the irregularly scattered woody plants in meadows and fields, boast a width of only a few yards. Just how wide a hedge may be while still being clearly discernable from small unpruned strips of bushes and small trees at field boundaries or from thickets in fields cannot be stated to the exact inch. Far more significant is the spatial structure of such an assemblage of woody plants, which results from the interaction of the soil, climate, economic conditions, and floristic composition of the region in question. Accordingly, we make a distinction between low hedges, high hedges, and hedges of trees.

A **low hedge** can be a stand composed predominantly of thornbushes (blackberry species, for example). Alternatively, it can be an older community of species, regularly coppiced (cut back to the stock) to provide a timber supply and exhibiting mature heights ranging from approximately 3 to 6.5 feet (1–2 m).

High hedges, in their undergrowth, contain the distinctive ensembles of species found in the low hedge, but they also include shrub species such as European elder, red dogwood, buckthorn, and hazel bush, which may possibly reach the 16-foot (5 m) mark and, in a few cases, even produce smallish trees.

Along pastures, the low shrub portion of the hedge can be heavily chewed by the grazing cattle and thus visibly reduced.

The **hedge of trees** includes shrubby woody plants and normal-sized trees such as common ash, common alder, hornbeam, hedge (field) maple, and English oak in groups or rows. In addition, it can be encased in a layer of low shrubs and a layer of tall shrubs.

The absolute measurements of these stands of woody plants are actually of minor importance. Much more decisive, along with their growth form, are the spatial distribution patterns in the open fields. Strips of woody plants, groups of shrubs, or mixed ensembles with single trees provide the agricultural landscape far and wide with vivid focal points, thus creating a near-natural organizational structure rich in texture and pattern.

The real significance of thickets, hedges, or woody species in fields lies in their function as a habitat. Every woody plant group made up of shrubs or a few trees within a hedge formation is a fascinating, complex microhabitat that, with its specific population of species, has an enriching and stabilizing effect on the neighboring areas.

Everywhere in Central Europe, manmade linear structures like paths, roads, railroad tracks, and electric power lines, as well as canals and other hydraulic constructions, have led to the division of almost all habitats into a great many parts. This process is known as insularization of the cultivated landscape. Hedges bring these islands back into a direct relationship.

In the photo: Shrub willows along bodies of running water help protect the bank. In earlier times, they supplied slender, pliant twigs (osiers) for basketwork or wickerwork.

Shrubs As a Habitat

In a stand of shrubs and trees that marks the boundary of a field or in a hedge border, two habitats with strongly contrasting structures meet one another. Ecologically, this situation is comparable to a woods' edge that borders directly on the open fields. Where the woodland ends and for example, the hay meadow or the root crop field begins, plants and animals of the woodland ecosystem encounter those of the agrarian ecosystem. Along with the inhabitants of these neighboring or interlocking habitats, there appear yet other groups of species that, in terms of their biotope requirements, have specialized precisely in the narrow boundary strips between the two worlds. The larger the number of differently structured and diverse partial habitats that collide in the rural landscape, and the more spatially effective their mutual boundary edges prove, the richer is the composition of their flora and fauna.

Woody Plants in Meadowlands

Stands of trees and shrubs in meadowlands are intermediate stations between woodlands and open fields belonging to a village community. In addition, they are independent edge systems with an independent population of species. Ecologically, the mixed stands of bushes and trees or the compact hedgerow could be understood as a very narrow, elongated forest that now consists exclusively of its edges, moved closer together, and that therefore manages to achieve an enormous number of species-promoting hemming-in effects in quite a small area.

To see this effect in quantitative terms you have only to wander through the meadows just after a snowfall and check to see where most of the animal tracks lead. Experience also shows that crows, jackdaws, pheasants, and the entire host of songbirds are most likely to be found in hedges and field margins consisting of woody plants, because that is where they find the cover they need and an abundance of food as well. Actually one ought to look at the relationships the other way around, and ask the critical question of how much open farm acreage the rural landscape can tolerate between the hedges and thickets and still remain ecologically intact to a defensible extent. Life is concentrated, so to speak, at the edge of hedges and/or in the immediate sphere of activity of shrubbery along field boundaries. More than 1,000 different animal species ranging from aphids to mammals inhabit these unique vital arteries of the countryside, living in and off them.

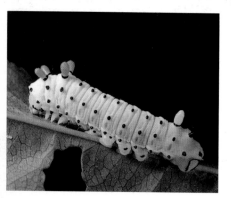

In the photos: Woody plants supply food and habitat for a great variety of animals.
The caterpillars of a moth (left) eat the leaves of woody species.
The common rabbit uses the base of a large shrub for housing and nesting sites.

Shelter and nesting area for many animals

Learning about shrubs

A wood mouse lays in a winter supply of hazelnuts

Shrubs for Animals

In populated areas and in the agrarian landscape in particular, shrubs and hedges have great significance as a habitat for wildlife, primarily for songbirds. While boughs and branches extend a year-round invitation to our feathered friends to perch and rest, leaf-covered shrubbery offers extremely attractive and highly coveted nesting sites. However, because individual shrubs and stands of shrubs vary widely in appearance they are not all equally suitable as cover for birds. Woody plants with densely branching tops and rampant, wide-spreading undergrowth are exceptionally good for nesting, provided the shrubs are not spaced too far apart. Hawthorn and sloe are more likely to possess those characteristics than alder buckthorn, elder, snowball bush, or wild rose. A detailed study has established that for every six-tenths of a

In the photo: Small animals derive a wide range of benefits from native shrubs. Chief among them are a nesting place and a supply of food.

mile (1,000 m) of hedgerow with optimal density, as many as 50 pairs of birds take up quarters. The age of the shrub population also plays a major role. Yellowhammers and greater whitethroats like to nest in shrubs that are at least five years old. Blackcap warblers and lesser whitethroats, as well as European thrushes, linnets, and red-backed shrikes, will readily accept both younger and distinctly older hedge plantings. Hedge sparrows, green linnets, chaffinches, and turtledoves prefer shrubs that are more than 20 years old. Many songbird species exhibit a clear preference for certain species of shrubs:

Shrubs and animals

Thrushes and green linnets like to brood in hawthorn bushes, while yellowhammers, hedge sparrows, and other warblers and whitethroats are more apt to choose densely branched sloe bushes.

Action on All Levels

The marginal situation in which bordering thickets, woody plants in fields, or a meadowland hedge exist brings together a great many species. If you examine one of these areas more closely you will see the extent to which such a stand of shrubs is actually the habitat of a wide variety of animal species. Songbirds or other bird species are perhaps the likeliest to attract attention. The blindworm or the grass frog, which hide in the undergrowth, are seen only in rare instances.

Even if a woody plant group in the open meadows at first seems very quiet and abandoned in fall or winter, it is nonetheless full of life. Many small animals have withdrawn into the ground layer of litter to hibernate. Others, including particularly the large numbers of hedge-dwelling insect groups, survive the adverse weather of the season as excellently camouflaged clutches of eggs in the crooks of branches, well-disguised or well-protected larvae in bark crevices, or as unobtrusive pupae hoping to escape the notice of hungry birds. Others, even fully developed insects, are able to cope with the uninviting conditions of the winter months. As early as the first sunny February days, one can see various insects in action in the hedge border: a brimstone butterfly or a painted lady, one or more bumblebees, or small swarms of dancing gnats. As spring and summer approach, the number of active species increases until it is no longer ascertainable. "Halfpints" like mites and aphids, as well as the curious gallwasps or gall gnats, beetles, butterflies, forest bees, dipterous insects, and numerous other tiny winged creatures stay in the various levels of a tiered border of woody plants. One or more large dragonflies on patrol flights often can be observed here in the summer, because the sphere of activity of a hedge border is inhabited by many incautious insects, which these skillful hunters and robbers can descend upon during flight and carry off.

Hedges and thickets are naturally also a thoroughly cobwebby world, in which round-web spiders and funnel weavers set up their snares. Especially on a late-summer morning fresh with dew, when thousands of glistening water droplets are hanging on the strands of outstretched cobwebs, it is easy to see how many small animals find their livelihood here—

In the photo: A bee pollinating a flower. The bright yellow flower parts provide visual attraction for many bees.

not counting the innumerable guests that come and go or stay only temporarily.

Microbiotope

Songbirds that rest in the boughs or simply come to keep a lookout for fat worms or juicy fruits are not permanently linked with a particular shrub. However, a shrub is equivalent to a habitat for very small creatures which spend the majority of their life cycle here. In such cases it is not the complete set of branches that is home to these diminutive animals, but only tiny portions of the total area of the shrub. One such example is insects that produce oddly shaped swellings on branches or leaves. The common rose gallwasp, by laying a single egg on native wild roses, stimulates the relevant plant tissue to abnormal growth by division. Within a short time (usually from June on), felt-like, globular structures arise, unlike any other organ of a rose. What from the outside appears to be a uniform structure is in reality a multichambered housing development. In each of the rounded chambers dwells a gallwasp larva that lives on plant matter, pupates after concluding its growth, and finally leaves the home of its youth as a complete insect, able to fly. New tenants may even settle down in the abandoned larval chamber—small insects that get none of their food

here, but find shelter and hiding places in nooks and crannies.

The small cracks, joints, rough places, and holes in the bark of many shrubs are, moreover, a clear invitation to other small creatures that are glad to gain a foothold here and, if possible, settle down permanently.

If you carefully strip off twigs or branches and end up with green stains on your fingers, you have visible evidence that minute microalgae also are part of the stem and branch population of a shrub. Usually these are thick deposits composed of vivid green-hued algae, which can proliferate even in pollutant-damaged sites affected by flue fumes and acid rain. Distant relatives of theirs, which also are classified as green algae but contain in addition a substantial quantity of bright yellow-red pigments, produce—especially in streamside shrubs of mountainous regions—conspicuous vermilion coatings.

Finally, many interesting lichens also can settle on the branches of old, gnarled shrubs in particular. The lichens do not harm their carrier plant, because they use it only as a permanent seat. In the case of European elder, for example, it is always worth searching for such unusual "squatters." Besides, you can also expect to find many mushrooms growing on these trees' outer bark, including the flesh-colored ear fungus and the intensely bright yellow tremella.

In contrast to the algae and lichens, most mushrooms do not live harmlessly on the outer bark, but are true parasites, depriving their host of all the substances they themselves require. Mushrooms growing

In the photo: In a few instances, imported shrub species also meet with the approval of wildlife. Greenfinches harvest the rose hips of the Japanese rose.

Life in the tiniest spaces

European cranberry bush in late fall, in fruit

on the bark usually send forth fungal threads (hyphae) into the living host tissue, to fill up with the sought-after substances. Often they lay the groundwork for other mushrooms that cause wood rot and hollow out stems or trunks. However, an ecological benefit is associated even with that, because many bird species, as hole-brooders, are dependent on rotted-out holes in stems, including those of relatively large shrub species.

However, often an exaggerated sense of tidiness gets in the way of our ability to appreciate the fact that dead wood and even rotten places in wood have an extremely valuable role in the diverse synergistic relationships involving shrubs and hedges. It is precisely the decayed and dead wood that shelters the larvae of insects that we later encounter as opalescent winged visitors alighting on our garden flowers.

In the photo: The harvest is far from over in fall. Fruit-bearing shrubs that retain their fruits in winter are important for roving birds.

Botanical Glossary

Accessory buds Additional buds next to the actual terminal or axillary bud, serving as a replacement in case of loss.

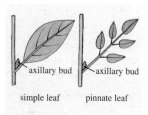

simple leaf   pinnate leaf

Aggregate fruit See Fruit Forms.

Alate, winged The shoot axis or the petiole has a narrow (green) border on both sides.

Alternate The leaves are located singly at a node.

Androgynous, bisexual The flower contains male (anthers) and female (ovaries) flower parts.

Anisophylly Leaves of different shapes or sizes at the same leaf node.

Anthers Pollen-containing parts of a stamen, usually consisting of two oblong cases and four pollen sacs.

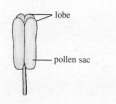

Ascending, ascendant Branches or stems that angle or curve from a horizontal position into a vertical one.

Axillary The flower or fruit is borne in the angle formed by the petiole and the axis of the shoot.

Axillary bud Bud in the angle formed by the petiole (leafstalk) and the axis of the shoot; often serves as a starting point for lateral branches.

Berry See Fruit Forms.

Blooming season Period from the unfolding of the flowers until flowering ceases. Early bloomers (hazel) flower long before the leaves are produced, while late bloomers (ivy) flower at the season's end.

Calyx Outer circle of the floral envelope, composed of green or occasionally also vividly hued sepals, which may be either separate or fused.

Capsule See Fruit Forms.

Climbing shrub Tall-growing, but not free-standing, woody plant that needs climbing supports or attaches itself to underlying surfaces.

Collective fruit See Fruit Forms.

Corymb, umbellike raceme See Types of Inflorescences.

Deciduous The plant retains its foliage only during the main vegetative period (from late March at the earliest to mid-November at the latest).

Decussate Opposite leaves, each pair of which is situated at a right angle to the pair at the node above or below.

Botanical glossary

Dehiscent fruit See Fruit Forms.

Dioecious Unisexual (male or female) flowers on separate individuals (gale, willows, juniper).

Drupe, stone fruit See Fruit Forms.

Endemite Species that occurs only in a very small, limited area.

Evergreen The plant bears broad-leaved foliage or needlelike foliage lasting for several years, often extremely long-lived.

Floral envelope, perianth Totality of the floral leaves (sepals and petals).

Follicle See Fruit Forms.

Fruit Flower or inflorescence in the state of ripeness, with all the organs that enclose the seed and serve to spread it.

Fruit forms

Simple fruits

Dehiscent fruits Split or burst open and discharge seeds passively

Follicle Many-seeded, derived from a single carpel (magnolia).

Pod Many-seeded, derived from two carpels (broom).

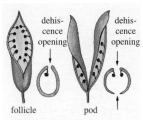

follicle   pod

Capsule Many-seeded, derived from several carpels (common heather, mountain rose).

capsule

Indehiscent fruits

Nut Usually one-seeded, with a firm wall (birch, alder).

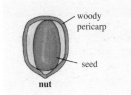

woody pericarp

seed

nut

Berry One- or many-seeded, with a juicy pericarp (barberry, blueberry).

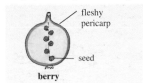

fleshy pericarp

seed

berry

Drupe, stone fruit One-seeded; the endocarp forms the stone (sloe, buckthorn, viburnum).

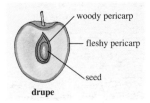

woody pericarp

fleshy pericarp

seed

drupe

Collective fruits, syncarps

Pome The floral axis, which becomes fleshy, surrounds the true fruit (core of apple and pear).

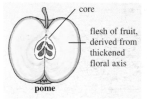

core

flesh of fruit, derived from thickened floral axis

pome

Aggregate fruit The spherical floral axis bears numerous small drupes or drupelets (blackberry, raspberry).

aggregate fruit

Hairs, pili Modifications of epidermal cells on the shoot axis or leaves; they can be branching or shieldlike and flat.

Botanical glossary

Heterophylly Differently shaped leaves at different leaf nodes, for example, on the climbing and the flowering shoots of ivy.

ivy leaf on climbing shoot ivy leaf on flowering shoot

Indehiscent fruit See Fruit Forms.

Inflorescence The part of the shoot axis system that bears the flowers.

Inner bark, phloem In contrast to the outermost layer (epidermis), the living part of the cortex, which attends to the conducting of organic substances.

Leaf Along with the root and the shoot axis, one of the three principal organs of a plant with a shoot; it arises from a leaf primordium with a ventral

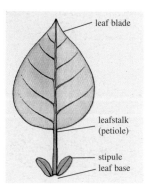

leaf blade

leafstalk (petiole)

stipule
leaf base

lobe (lower part) and an epiphyll. The ventral lobe supplies the leaf base (with the leaf sheath or stipules), while the epiphyll supplies the petiole and the flat-spread leaf blade.

Leaf tips
[see drawing captions]

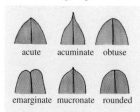

acute   acuminate   obtuse

emarginate mucronate rounded

Leaf margins
[see drawing captions]

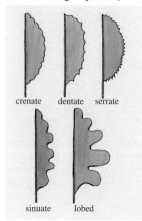

crenate   dentate   serrate

sinuate   lobed

Leaf shapes
[see drawing captions]

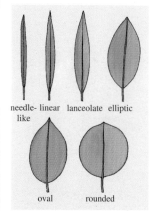

needle- linear lanceolate elliptic
like

oval   rounded

Leaf thorns Thorns that were formed from leaf primordia.

Leaf veins Conduction paths for transportation of substances; they run from the shoot axis through the petiole into the leaf blade (lamina) and also serve to stiffen the leaf.

Monoecious Unisexual (male or female) flowers on the same individual (hazel).

Nut See Fruit Forms.

Botanical glossary

Opposite Leaves in pairs, one on either side of the same node.

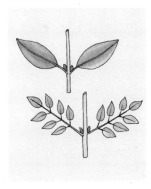

Panicle See Types of Inflorescences.

Perennial Herbaceous or woody plant that lives several to many years.

Perianth Consists of the calyx (sepals) and the corolla (petals).

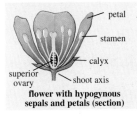

flower with hypogynous sepals and petals (section)

Perigonium Special form of the floral envelope, in which the calyx and the corolla are indistinguishable in both shape and color.

Phenology The course of the phenomena of life (foliation, flowering, ripening of fruit) of a plant during the year;

useful in determining the biological calendar and describing the climate.

Photosynthesis Important metabolic process in the plant, in which the green pigment (chlorophyll), using energy from sunlight, makes sugar and other organic substances out of water and carbon dioxide.

Pinnate leaf Compound leaf consisting of a leaf vein or rachis and several leaflets (pinnae). Imparipinnate leaves terminate in a leaflet; paripinnate leaves end with the rachis.

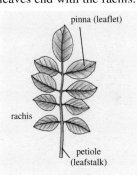

Pod See Fruit Forms.

Pollen Microspores or grains that originate in the anthers and are transferred during pollination.

Pollination Transfer of pollen grains by wind or animals from the anthers of Flower A to the stigma of Flower B on another individual of the same species.

Pome See Fruit Forms.

Raceme See Types of Inflorescences.

Rounded See Leaf Shapes.

Seed Propagation and dissemination unit of the seed plants (flowering plants); derived from a fertilized ovule and consists of an embryo and an endosperm, which are surrounded by a protective seedcoat (testa).

Sessile The leaf blade is borne on the shoot axis, with no discernible stalk.

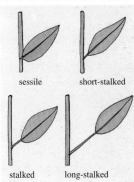

Semi-evergreen Woody plants that generally retain their (usually annual) leaves until spring.

Shade tree Tolerates temporary or constant shade from a taller-growing stand.

Shoot General structural model of a plant that consists of roots, a shoot axis, and leaves.

Shoot axis Above-ground, woody or nonwoody, leaf-bearing parts of a plant; also commonly referred to as the stem.

Shooting forth, putting forth Development of the buds and beginning of the longitudinal growth of the shoot axis.

Shrub Free-standing woody plant, usually with several main stems, and having no clear trunk length.

Simple fruit See Fruit Forms

Species A group of plant (and animal) organisms that correspond in all essential characteristics, occupy a joint geographic range, and are potentially able to interbreed within the group.

Spike See Types of Inflorescences.

Stalk, stem Usually non-woody, above-ground part of the shoot; it is divided into nodes and internodes.

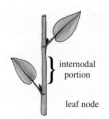

internodal portion

leaf node

Stem thorns Sharp, very rigid, and often unbranched structures that arise through modification of stem (shoot) ends (as in the case of sloe).

Subshrub Free-standing, usually multi-stemmed plant, generally woody only at its base.

Tendrils Specialized organs of the shoot axis, with which climbing plants anchor themselves to supporting surfaces—for example, by means of petioles that creep (clematis) or tendril-like structures that are morphologically stems (grapevine, Virginia creeper).

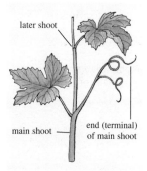

later shoot

main shoot

end (terminal) of main shoot

Terminal, apical The flower or fruit is borne at the end of a main or secondary axis.

Thorns, spines Pointed, piercing components of the shoot axis that are not easy to detach; usually arising through modification of leaves or ends of shoot axes.

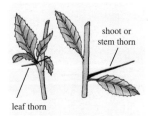

shoot or stem thorn

leaf thorn

Botanical glossary

Tree line Climatic limit beyond which tree growth is no longer possible.

Tube Closely united, cylindrical part of a calyx or a corolla.

Tree Large, self-supporting woody plant, usually with a single trunk.

Types of inflorescences

Corymb The flowers of a raceme, with pedicels of unequal length, are borne at a common level.

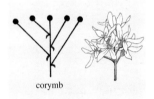

corymb

Panicle A raceme with compound branching and a terminal flower.

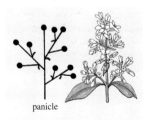

panicle

Raceme Stalked single flowers in the axil of subtending leaves.

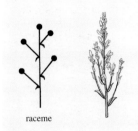

raceme

Spike Several stalkless flowers on one axis.

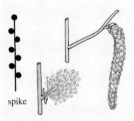

spike

Umbel Compressed raceme; pedicels (flower-stalks) arise from a common point.

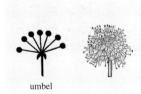

umbel

Umbel See Types of Inflorescences.

Unisexual, diclinous The flower contains only male (anthers) or female (ovaries) flower parts.

Verticillate More than two leaves are located at the same node (whorled).

Whorled More than two leaves are borne at the same node (verticillate).

Wood Cell unions or tissues that become very firm and stable through depositing of lignin.

Woody, lignified Cell unions or tissues that have become very firm and stable through deposition of lignin.

Zygomorphic, irregular The flower is bilaterally symmetrical (broom, laburnum); that is, only one (vertical) axis of symmetry is possible.

Historic cultivated land: The dwarf shrub/juniper stands of the Lüneburg Heath developed as a result of human economic activity.

Experiencing Shrubs

As components of nature's green backdrop, shrubs play an extremely important role, both in the woods and fields, and near houses, in parks, and in gardens as well. Wild shrubs border the edges of forests and the banks of bodies of water, provide the open meadows with agreeable focal points consisting of little islands of common woody plants and strips of thicket; and stand at the sides of paths and roads to serve as green guidelines. Ornamental shrubs, frequently native to other countries, delight the senses with their brilliant colors, magnificent fragrances, and handsome fruits.

Throughout the year, from the time the leaves are produced until they fall, there is always something to discover and to experience—if you only look closely enough. Shrubs are lovely and extremely picturesque ingredients of our environment. It is worthwhile knowing and learning more about them.

Shrubs over the Course of the Year

We pay them little notice as long as green or multicolored leaves are still attached to a woody plant. On winter's bare boughs, however, they are more likely to attract attention. But ever since the final weeks of summer, they've been here: the winter buds.

Winter—Leaves and Flowers Well Wrapped Up

Winter buds are an often overlooked, but tremendously important, special article of equipment at the ends of branches. They have a surprisingly large number of remarkable properties that are ingeniously tied into the seasonal course of events. In many areas, in fall and winter, the ambient temperatures sink gradually and inexorably into the neighborhood of the freezing point. Most woody plants no longer can afford to bear succulent and therefore quite vulnerable foliage that constantly transpires water over its large surface area. When the upper soil layers freeze and, to make things even worse, snow falls, vitally necessary water becomes an exceedingly scarce commodity for the woody plants. The scarcity of water is magnified as the plants are faced with the problem of having to transport it from the roots over fairly long distances to the places of consumption at the tips of the branches. The sole ecologically appropriate response to the frosty aspects of winter weather proves to be simultaneously a physiologically brilliant, perhaps even perfect, solution. In the cold season, the leaves, which have a high rate of transpiration and are constantly endangered by frost, are simply shed. While small shrubs can hug the ground or at least rely on the protection of a sufficiently deep snow cover, taller-growing shrubs and trees simply pin their hopes on winter buds—small, compact, tightly closed parcels, rich in content and equipped with an unbelievably fine-tuned program of development.

Does the Bud Covering Give Thermal Protection?

Although the bud covering surrounds the leaf primordia and the early developmental stages of flowers with multiple layers, it nevertheless affords no thermal protection. It doesn't require days of freezing temperatures for it to be exactly as cold inside the bud as a few millimeters outside it, in the open air. Therefore, the bud coverings are not a warming winter coat, although the extremely firm, coarse-shelled protective bud scales may suggest this at first.

Protection of the sensitive, ready-to-develop tissue against harmful frostbite is indispensable, however, and it is supplied—just as in a car's radiator water—by special antifreezing agents such as sugars and amino acids, stored in the cells. In addition, the tissues have a very low water content during the winter rest period.

Keeping Water Out and In

If the bud covering is not there to protect against cold, it must have a totally different task assigned to it. Besides affording a certain mechanical protection of the bud's inner life, the horny outer scales

In the photos: Because buds are so changeable, a shrub often can be identified in winter on the basis of the way its buds look. Here, only a small selection.

Various bud shapes

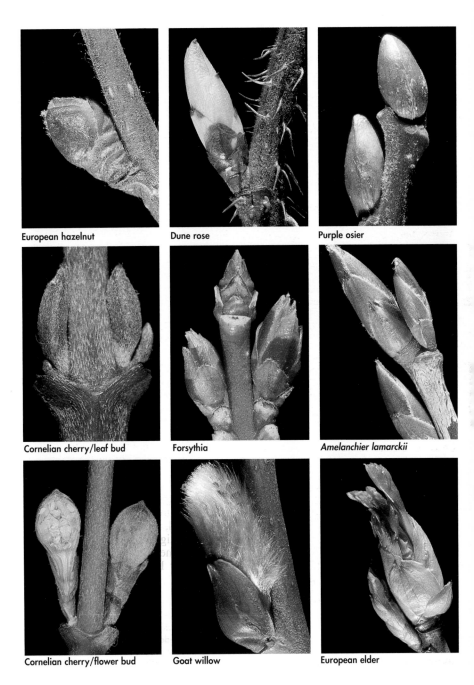

European hazelnut

Dune rose

Purple osier

Cornelian cherry/leaf bud

Forsythia

Amelanchier lamarckii

Cornelian cherry/flower bud

Goat willow

European elder

Experiencing shrubs

European hazel bush in spring

primarily prevent unregulated water exchange between the dormant organ rudiments and the environment. Despite extensive curtailments, the tissues of the rudimentary flowers and leaves concealed in the buds still contain small amounts of residual water, without which they simply cannot get by. The coarse covering effectively prevents the transpiration of the remaining water in the tissue.

Just as harmful would be a premature and unregulated swelling of the buds during thawing periods that last for days, with mild temperatures clearly above 32° F (0° C). Then, when frost sets in again, dangerous ice crystals could form quickly and would irreparably destroy the fine structures of the leaf primordia. When snowfall and continuous frost are followed by a few sunny days with early spring temperatures, little torrents of water course through the branches. The

In the photos: Early bloomers like the European hazel bush produce their flowers long before the leaves (above). Because insects are not yet active at this time, the plants simply toss their masses of pollen grains to the winds. The leaves do not push their way out of the protective buds (below) until some weeks later.

Nonreturnable packaging

In the photo: Winter or snow heath does great credit to its name. It flowers as early as late winter, even when covered with snow.

bud scales—which may be brown or yellow, covered with a whitish-gray frostlike bloom, or even purple-red—have to bulkhead off this water. For that purpose, their margins in some cases are covered in addition with water-repelling hairs or even sealed all around with a tough, gummy material.

Winter buds are a theme with a great many variations. Along with a sizable palette including some rather showy colors, they amaze us with the great variety of their shapes and structures. Some buds have only two or three (outwardly visible) protective scales, arched like a hood, while others have multipartite, fishbone-like sets of scales. Some leaf or flower buds nestle tightly against the branch, while others stand far away. Often the particular bud shape can be used as a basis for predicting whether the series of scales conceals only leaf primordia or the early developmental stages of flowers or perhaps both.

Winter buds are so diverse in design that a great many shrub species can be accurately identified solely on the basis of the way their specific buds look.

Terminal, Axillary, or Replacement Buds
With many shrubs, apical growth is dominant. The terminal buds of the branches get a much bigger push in their development than the axillary (lateral) buds that are next in order, and for this reason they look correspondingly luxuriant—as in lilac, for example. The axillary and accessory buds can quickly make up for their obvious lag in development if the terminal bud should be lost—falling victim, for example, to bud-eating birds like hawfinches, which are not deterred even by the bitter-tasting resin of the multilayered bud covering. The accessory buds, therefore, also serve as reservists, able if need be to wait years for the call to active duty. Forsythias, for example, exhibit whole series of accessory or replacement buds.

Surprisingly, some shrubby woody plants also manage without the protection of tightly closed buds. In the European elder, the bare leaf primordia gape out of the few bud scales practically all winter long.

Spring—the Wrappings Come Off
As spring approaches, the sunlight and warmth provide an enormous amount of development aid. Most woody plants that are leafless in winter need only about two weeks to turn green. The step toward unfolding the summer foliage cannot be taken without thorough advance prepara-

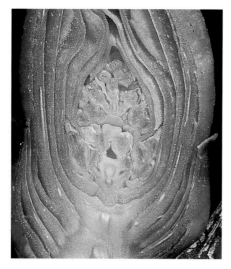

In the photo: The lilac bud is a miracle. Besides the unopened but already green leaves, the bud also contains the inflorescence, still very compact.

inhibitor hormone decrease, while a different, growth-promoting factor with the opposite effect steadily increases. In spring, when frost is less likely, the buds are ready at last: A few warm, sunny days finally put an end to their winter rest.

The Buds Break Open

Before the first green leaf tips become visible in their protective packaging, the young tissue pumps itself full of water. Development and unfolding require energy and material, of course, and both processes can be accomplished only by rapid mobilization of substances held in reserve. However, without water the entire series of reactions involving conversion and redistribution of materials would not be possible. As they take on water, the buds swell visibly. They stretch out and enlarge their volume many times over. Before the new leaf forces its way out of its safe winter hiding place, the protective bud scales have become considerably longer. The assemblage of scales, at first tightly closed all around, begins to loosen row by row. Only because the scales and the young leaf organs for some time continue to grow in a common lengthwise direction is it possible for enough room to become available inside the bud to permit further development of the fresh summer foliage. The winter bud covering is not simply blasted away. Neither is the thrilling process of the bud's opening comparable to the shattering of the eggshell when a chick hatches. Rather, the protective wrappings gradually swivel to the side when the spring growth occurs, steadily and carefully exposing the tender young green to the fresh air.

tion, however. A great many finely synchronized processes mesh during this process.

Each bud already has done the most important part of its job: Inside the winter buds, packed in thick scale leaves, are almost completely developed leaves and flowers that were begun as long ago as the final weeks of the previous year's season. They now are squeezed together in a tiny space, and for that reason alone they have not yet grown to their final size. Everything a leaf requires, however, was already prepared in detail during the late summer and fall of the preceding year: the leafstalk, the leaf blade, the hairs on the leaf's surface, the leaf venation, and, moreover, even a little touch of green pigment.

In the cold months of the year, a high level of certain inhibitors in the tissue of the leaf primordia ensures that the necessary, climate-related period of dormancy is actually observed. Only during the late winter, under the influence of cold temperatures and increasingly long days, does the concentration of the plant's

Stretching and pushing

In many woody plants, the markedly lengthened bud scales continue to cling to the branches for quite some time after the leaves have unfolded. Not until April or May do they fall to the ground. At the base of every year's growth, the bud scales leave behind tiny scars, which are still visible even many years later and that mark the boundaries of the annual growth of the previous years. Thus you can very easily determine the age of a branch or stem by counting the bud scale scars.

The Leaves Unfold

Soon after the buds open, the final shape of the leaf is discernible. It already has all the typical characteristics of the species. The roughly six million cells of which the leaf of a hazel bush, for example, is composed, are already complete. The entire impressive spectacle of leaf production and the concomitant greening of the shrubs consists from now on of a further increase in the size of the leaf cells, already present in full number.

Even after the unfolding, you can clearly tell by looking at many foliage leaves how they were positioned inside the bud. The leaves of birch, hazel, and alder appear in a mixture of transverse and longitudinal folds. Many leaves never manage to iron out the wrinkles of their youth and look crumpled all their lives. Other leaves, like those of willow or crab apple, lie rolled up in the bud, because their surfaces and undersides do not evolve equally strongly at first. Only subsequent development during the leaf flush largely makes up for these differences. Some species turn their leaf margins downward or, for better protection against transpiration, stay fairly tightly rolled.

Early Summer—Blossom Time

Although it sometimes doesn't look that way, the flowers of the shrubs also consist exclusively of specially tailored leaves, each perfectly adapted to its particular set task. This modification can be so extreme that almost nothing about the finished petal reminds us of its original nature as a leaf.

Basically, the same sequence of special leaf organs can be identified in every flower, going from outside toward the center. In the outermost layer (or at the very bottom) are the sepals. They are followed by the petals. In most instances, the sepals and the petals together form a double floral envelope, or perianth, consisting of two leaf layers and constituting the "wrapping material" of the actual reproductive organs. For reproduction, both stamens and carpels are necessary. Both are present in large numbers.

By and large, all flowers conform to this basic plan of construction. However, Mother Nature repeatedly has altered the basic concept of the flower in a variety of ways and developed models so different in appearance that virtually every plant species has received its own typical flower design.

Delicate or Magnificent

In the life of woody plants too, flowers are the first of many stages in the propagative program. The most important goals, which are achievable while the

blooming season is still under way, are the transfer of pollen (pollination) and the fertilization of the ovules. Without these processes, no seed can form and no fruit can ripen.

The shrubs also have two means of transferring the pollen grains from one flower to another: Either they consign their pollen to the wind and let the air currents carry it over long distances, or they use many kinds of promotional offers to entice animals and insects to visit the flower, and then leave the pollen transport to them. Normally you can tell by looking at flowers whether they employ the wind or the flying insects as pollinators.

Wind-pollinated flowers exhibit no eye-catching packaging of any kind, and in terms of their structure and accessories they restrict themselves to the essentials. Their flower design, too, is generally quite simplified. Examples are sea buckthorn (see page 104), sweet gale (see page 160), and dwarf birch (see page 163). That does not mean, however, that these flowers have no special adaptations. In the case of downy oak (see page 161) or hazel (see page 164), the male inflorescences (catkins) hang loosely in the wind and enable the millions of falling pollen grains to get the best possible start on their journey through the air. On the receiving side, too, special precautions have been taken: The female stigmas of wind-pollinated (anemophilous) species

In the photos: In comparison with the large male catkins, the crimson female flowers of the hazel bush are very small. Both are borne separately on the same shrub (monoecious). The handsome flowers of chaenomeles (right) are bisexual. Our eyes are not alone in succumbing to their visual lure.

Goat willow, male catkin

Purple osier, male catkin

Purple osier, male catkin

are almost always especially large and, moreover, they lean far out of their inflorescences so that the chances for snaring the flying pollen grains are correspondingly improved.

Plants that are pollinated by animals, by contrast, make their flowers into real ornaments: Brilliant colors, lush shapes, and ideal placing are the most conspicuous features. With their flowers, which often are even garish in color, many woody plants also engage in a lot of ballyhoo and self-promotion. Precisely for these reasons, they also are very popular as ornamental or flowering shrubs in parks and gardens.

Floral Architecture

For reasons of special functional adaptation, the flowers of the anemophilous species are heavily simplified, rather small and unassuming, and very frequently even incompletely developed. By contrast, in large plants pollinated by animals—for example, in the wild rose or the blackberry—the basic plan of floral structure, with the sepals, petals, stamens, carpels sequence, is much more distinct and clearly discernible.

The sepals are generally small, green, and unobtrusive. In many shrubs, they even contribute to the often showy overall appearance of the flower. In the *Clematis* species, the large and obvious leaves of the floral envelope are in reality sepals that are very much on the sumptuous side, while the actual corolla is absent. We find similar circumstances in the

In the photos: The flowers of wind-pollinated plants, like the willow catkins shown here, can also be very decorative. When they bloom (center and bottom), the catkins change color.

Flowers—morphological groups

Bee paying a visit to the inflorescence of a member of the sunflower family

flowers of the *Daphne* species. In many members of the heath family (Ericaceae)—in heather, for example—the sepals are vividly colored and thus support the color effect of the corolla.

Quite independently of the size, colorfulness, and number of the petals, the flowers of the shrubs can be divided into two groups of forms on the basis of the shape of their corolla. The floral cross section resembles either that of dog rose and bush cinquefoil or that of Judas tree and Scotch broom. The differences obviously affect the floral symmetry.

In the rose family (Rosaceae), the colored petals are arranged like the spokes of a wheel or the points of a star—you can divide them into congruent halves through several planes of symmetry. For this reason, they are described as radially symmetrical.

However, with the Papilionaceae, only the right and the left halves of the flower are congruent, while the upper and the lower halves are not. Such flowers are described as zygomorphic, or bilaterally symmetrical (like a mirror image). These flowers often look far more bizarre and decorative than the little star-shaped flowers, which are a great deal simpler in effect and always seem a little aimless.

Single Flowers and Large Bouquets

Amazingly few flowering shrubs content themselves with lifting a single, especially lovely flower on an elongated stalk into the limelight or, like twinflower, with developing a double solution, with two flowers on a stalk. The great majority of the shrubs bundle and bunch their flowers into relatively large inflorescences, to give you an even better view of the mar-

Experiencing shrubs

Early azalea flowers

velous white or rose-pink flowers of the individual species of woody plants.

There are several technical possibilities for the structure of the inflorescences. Almost all inflorescences can be assigned to one of these few basic patterns. (The less common special cases are not covered in this discussion.)

Many sessile single flowers on one elongated stalk are known as a **spike**. In woody plants, this inflorescence occurs primarily in the form of **catkins**. If the flowers clearly have stalks, the inflorescence is called a **raceme**, and if the flowerstalks all originate at a common point on the main axis, the inflorescence in question is an **umbel**. A **panicle** differs from a raceme in that the individual flowers are borne at the ends of branching lateral axes. From above, a **corymb** looks like an umbel, but from the side it quite

clearly exhibits the typical branching pattern of a panicle.

Among the shrubs, there also occur unusually shaped inflorescences that look like a single large superflower—and also behave accordingly. One impressive example is the European cranberry bush *(Viburnum opulus)*. Its inflorescence consists largely of numerous small single flowers, but also includes especially large, glorious marginal (ray) flowers that make the entire corymb appear to be a single flower made up of many parts. In the hydrangeas, too, we find this same purposeful optical illusion.

48

Flowers with operating instructions

In the photo: Barberry flowers are very rich in nectar. The stamens fold inward when touched (right, below), and the head of the insect that triggered that response is covered with pollen.

Alluring Splendor

Before insects rush busily from flower to flower, transferring pollen grains all the while, an eminently practical problem has to be solved: How does a certain plant species induce a bee, bumblebee, butterfly, or fly to dispatch pollen from Flower A to Flower B? Certainly, these animals do not accept their special freight orders unselfishly. Conveying pollen, strictly speaking, is an outcome that the flowers' winged visitors do not even notice. The animal air fleet's interest in the flowers is much more superficial: Bees, beetles, syrphid flies, and other "tiny winged creatures" go to a flower only because they have something to gain there. Nectar glands, concealed at various places in the flowers, produce a highly concentrated sugar solution in large quantities. Many flowers offer their nectar without ceremony. In barberry and mahonia, the entire receptacle fairly drips with sugar water. Other flowers, with a narrow cylindrical structure (woodbine honeysuckle, for example), admit only special visitors— particularly butterflies.

Flowers offer their visitors more than nectar, however. Animals that are reluctant to eat a steady diet of the highly concentrated solution also find a variety of other things to snack on. Some flowers serve nothing less than pollen grains to their hotly courted visitors—solid food intended for shipment to other flowers of the same species. Roses and blackberries, as well as traveler's joy and the hypericum species, are such flowers. They make pollen available literally by the sackful. You can recognize most of the insects that make a stop at that kind of pollen-dusty eatery: The ones that actually sat down there are dusted with yellow or white when they fly away.

Navigational Aids and Guidelines

No snack bar can get by without advertising, and that is all the more true for a countryside restaurant. That is precisely the reason that the originally simple flowers became surpassingly attractive blossoms that excite attention with all kinds of optical (and aromatic) means. A spot of color on a neutral green background alone arouses ample curiosity and also attracts winged visitors in large numbers. In its overall visual appearance, however, a flower is far more than a mere eye-catcher. Flowers also provide their visitors with a great deal of pertinent information. If you are thirsty or hungry, for example, and head for a restaurant, you don't want to have to spend time hunting for the entrance. That is why the flowers show their visitors the right way, by means of the difference in color between the center of the flower and the periphery. These kinds of contrastive schemes, which lead the approaching insect accurately to the center (where the entrance to the stores of nectar usually is located), have an effect on us as well. Almost as a matter of course, our glances are literally drawn to the geometric center of a flower. Special patterns of lines and dots reinforce this effect. They are found on the standards (vexillae) of the Papilionaceae—for example, Scotch broom, laburnum, sage, or rose of Sharon.

Once the external features of flower design have brought the urgently needed pollen couriers up close successfully, then additional refinements of the individual organs ensure that the visitors actually get enough pollen on them. A bumblebee that rolls around in a rose blossom usually churns up enough pollen to cover its wool with an adequate load for the next target flower. However, if the flower is especially narrow—as in the case of the Ericaceae—and not enough pollen trickles toward the bumblebee, the flower provides a little assistance. Rapid vibrations of the bumblebee's flight muscles produce high-frequency tones, which the stamens find so moving that a larger helping of pollen grains immediately starts to slide. If a relatively heavy insect sits on the flowers of Scotch broom, the involuted stamens thrust forward with lightning speed, almost giving the visitor a hook to the chin and liberally covering the insect's body with pollen. With sage, the pair of anthers drops down like a barrier when touched, while with bladder senna the flower acts as a brush, sweeping a healthy load of pollen into the wool of each guest.

Fall—Season of Ripening Fruit

Shrubs also are by no means content with only the site that they happen to occupy at the moment. As soon as the blooming season is over, they try to overcome even fairly large distances by means of abundant fruit and seed production, in order to conquer other biotopes located far away for their own use. All sorts of ingenious procedures—from flying carpets to alluring fruits—are employed for the purpose of spreading throughout a larger area.

Basically the woody plants have two methods of dispatching their fruits or seeds on as distant a journey as possible. Either they simply fling everything (fruits and/or seeds) to the winds, or they literally cast down their fruits, along with the enclosed seeds, for the animals to eat.

In the photo: The flowers of some imported shrub species—here, those of spike winter hazel—often arouse no interest at all in native insects.

Roving far afield

Fruits of white dryas

Thrown to the Winds

For wind dissemination to occur, seeds and fruits have to meet special technical prerequisites: They need to be as small and as light as possible. Before they begin their air journey, therefore, they surrender their water ballast and become dry enough to crackle. That reduces their takeoff weight. Many seeds are constructed in an extremely material-efficient way as well—even seeds of large woody plants can be extremely tiny. Good examples are all our shrub willows, whose seeds are far smaller than the head of a pin. Supported by fine, silky hull fibers that catch every breath of air, they are already drifting about in dense clouds by early summer. Often the hull fibers of several such seeds get stuck together and resemble small flying carpets. Thus it is understandable that their range can cover dozens of miles and that some woody species are always the first on the scene as pioneer plants whenever it is a question of occupying virgin soils or other newly available environments.

In the photo: Fruits that are disseminated by airmail develop particularly lightweight flying organs for their single journey by air.

The lightweight birch nutlets also cover substantial flying distances. Subtended by foliaceous bracts, they fly over the countryside like frisbees that have been tossed in large numbers. On the whole, apart from the members of the willow and birch families, relatively few of the shrubby woody plants are equipped for wind dispersal. This particular means of dissemination is far more common among tree species. The reason obviously is that the air travelers among the seeds and fruits cannot expect ideal takeoff conditions from the low-growing shrubs. Therefore, the propeller-assisted gliders (like the fruits of maple, for example), whose operations cover shorter distances in any event, on the whole are not associated with shrubs.

Experiencing shrubs

In the photo: Fascinating for birds' eyes: opened capsular fruit of warty spindle tree, with showy red seedcoat and black seed.

Animals as Spreaders of Seeds

Among the seeds and fruits there also are some real heavyweights—just think of hazelnuts, for example, or the acorns of the shrub oaks. Wind dissemination is out of the question here, naturally, but nonetheless there are superbly functioning channels of distribution for these chubby fruits, which hit the ground with a thud. Now animals appear on the scene. Because of their high nutrient content, it is the somewhat more amply proportioned seeds and fruits that are distinctly popular with animals—it is the reason they are gathered, to be eaten at once or stored as a reserve supply. Squirrels and jays set up several depots in fall, many of them right in the ground, to consolidate the foods they gather from distant sources. One jay, over the course of a single month, can transport hundreds of hazelnuts or acorns. Some of these stores are actually consumed by the hungry animals during the winter weeks, but others are simply forgotten. Thus all the participants benefit: The surplus feeds the animals, and the remainder—carried away, buried, and forgotten—ensures sufficient new growth of woody plants in all kinds of places.

Many woody plants also promote their fruits with colors that have great appeal.

The target group of the juicy berries and lush drupes consists of various small mammals and, above all, birds, which respond especially well to shades of red. Birds are also quick to discover the dark blue fruits or those covered with a gray-blue frostlike bloom, although these hues seem rather like camouflage colors to us. The waxy coating is especially good at reflecting short-wave light, to which birds' eyes are highly receptive. The rather inconspicuous fruits of blue honeysuckle, dewberry, and sloe look especially brilliant and inviting to them for that reason.

The feathered creatures do not always get the complete harvest in during the first few weeks of fall. Frequently, fairly large supplies remain on the branches for several months to come. These are the so-called "winter stayers," or seeds or fruits retained by plants through winter. All birds that remain here in winter or come from areas farther north fall back upon these reserves eagerly. For the migratory birds returning from the warm southern regions in the spring, too, these fruits are in some cases a very important food supply. However, by the time the new season begins, the dried fruit and winter fruit will long since be used up and gone.

Although the animals consume the fruits, the plants concerned are guaranteed successful dispersal because the seeds, which mostly are very hard-shelled and hence indigestible, survive passage through the gastrointestinal tract completely unharmed and without any loss in germination capacity. On the contrary, many seeds are able to germinate only after they have spent a certain time in the digestive tract of a bird. In many plant

Dried and frozen fruits

Fall foliage changes after the first frost

species, the surrounding fruit pulp contains germination-inhibiting substances, whose retarding effect is relaxed only by the digestive enzymes of the fruit-eating animals.

Winter Approaches—Lots of Falling Leaves

Colors almost always play a role in the lives of plants: Flowers attract pollinating insects by means of extremely decorative make-up. A great many fruits also use showy, hard-to-miss colors as an effective advertising ploy. But in the case of fall foliage, when the leaves of the deciduous shrubs and trees are unexcelled in their glory, the lavish blaze of color has no specific signals to give.

The deciduous broad-leaved woody plants bring the months of growing, blooming, and ripening to an end with a skillful finale. Every stretch of woodland

In the photo: Often, brightly colored fruits remain after leaf fall.

and every island of woody plants in fields and meadows presents an exceptionally impressive pageant from late September to November. An amazingly comprehensive palette of colors is on display, ranging from vivid ochre through various shades of yellow and brown to flaming crimson. Once the shrubs and trees are clad in their fall leaves, the entire landscape suddenly has a different face. Where flowers and fruits are concerned, the meaning of the striking colors can be summarized clearly and plainly: The intent is to lure insects for pollination and to disperse the seeds or fruits—functions that clearly serve the purposes of propagation and dissemination. Colorful

Experiencing shrubs

Showing its true colors: Virginia creeper in splendid fall hues

autumn leaves no longer have anything at all to do with reproduction, however.

In fact, the leaves' vivid change of color is only a particularly splendid requiem that is presented shortly before they fall. For that reason, colorful autumn foliage is to be expected only in woody plants that lose their leaves annually. In evergreen shrubs, the occasional replacement of the leaves takes place very unobtrusively and almost always without any sizable or noticeable orgies of color.

Securing Whatever Can Be Salvaged

Unless woody plants are evergreen, they treat their summer leaves like disposable articles that are worn out after a single season. On the other hand a certain amount of material resources had to be utilized for the development, growth, and equipment of the seasonal leaves. For that reason, even before the shrubs bid

In the photo: The brilliant coloring of fall leaves, which progresses to the saturation point, is an indication of dramatic metabolic processes in the leaf tissues. The plant does not derive any particular benefit from its splendid colors.

farewell to their leaves during the weeks of autumn, they withdraw all usable substances from the worn-out leaf organs and store them in the xylem for reuse—recycling of materials to perfection.

Among the especially valuable components of the leaves are their green pigments. Consequently they are the first to be withdrawn, so that the yellow pigments which still are present stand out all the more noticeably. From time to time woody plants in fall also engage in an appreciable new synthesis of pigments,

Riot of color at the season's end

In the photo: Depending on the species, the fall leaves produce a variety of tints ranging from intense crimson to brilliant gold-yellow (as here, in this witch hazel). Weather conditions on fall days influence these processes.

especially of water-soluble substances with a distinctly yellow-red or bright red hue. When the autumn wind gets into the boughs and loosens the leaves from the stems, in most cases it is only comparatively worthless packaging that falls to the ground.

Naturally, the deciduous woody plants have to begin their fall metamorphosis at the right time. They react to a signal that appears every year in the same way: the decreasing length of the days. When the days begin to grow perceptibly shorter from September on, the trees and shrubs automatically get ready to shed their leaves. They set in motion the resource-conserving process of recovering materials, produce special isolating tissue at the petiole, and in this way also switch off the water supply of the leaves—a sequence of different operations that have to be well coordinated with one another. The exposure meters needed for discerning the shortening days of autumn are the leaves themselves. Along streets and in brightly lit areas, deciduous woody plants sometimes are fooled. In these locations, streetlights artificially keep them under long-day conditions. For shrubs with a continuously prolonged period of illumination, mid-October is still the middle of summer. Consequently, within the range of powerful streetlights or front yard lights their leaves show very little inclination to change color or fall to the ground. They stay green until the first nighttime frosts force them to give up once and for all.

It is fascinating to take a closer look at the lovely color patterns of the leaves in their autumn hues and to compare the various possibilities. Some leaves change color from the margins toward the principal veins. In other leaves, the leaf tissues take the opposite path and begin withdrawing substances and changing color at the center. Sometimes normal green spots, like islands, remain in a leaf that otherwise has changed color uniformly. Here the metabolic processes in the leaf have been disturbed, by miner insect larvae or fungi, for example. Such areas of the leaf are completely unaware that fall arrived a long time ago.

Leaf Utilizers

The autumn leaves are barely on the ground before an army of tiny organisms attacks this biomass, breaks it up until it is no longer recognizable, and finally breaks it down into the original materials. These infinitely important organisms are called destruents by ecologists. Their specific industrial material is the now-faded summer wardrobe of the woody plants: the huge mass of nonreturnable leaves,

55

Experiencing shrubs

Pitting

Tunnels of miner larvae

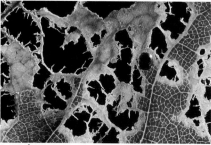

Insect damage

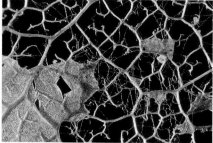

Skeletonized leaf

dead pieces of stems, worn-out pericarps, and whatever else has to make way for the new growth of the coming season. Professionals use the term detritus to refer to the cast-offs of the shrubs and trees. The elegance of the word suggests that waste by no means has to be synonymous with trash.

Fallen leaves do not lie on the ground indefinitely—their decomposition takes place in installments. First, an armada of large and small inhabitants of the leaf litter advances, merely gnawing a little at the leaves. Wood lice, ringed worms, bristletails, earwigs, springtails, and beetle mites are the members of the first column. By randomly eating holes in the leaves, they first give themselves access to the deeper-lying leaf tissues and devour the relatively soft parts. Large numbers of insect larvae, including those of March flies, crane flies, fickle midges, and ibis flies, now get their share as well. Soon the once beautiful leaf is nothing more than a skeleton. There remain only the offshoots of the quite rigid, hard leaf veins, which for the time being still withstand the bite of the destruents, or detritivores. Seen against the light, the leaf veins create especially bizarre, beautifully patterned structures that are slightly reminiscent of the intricate decorations of Baroque wrought-iron work.

But this splendid design too is only temporarily a miniature work of art. Someday, other small organisms and microorganisms will take a fancy to the long-since abandoned leaf infrastructures, until only crumbly, almost amorphous humus is left.

In the photos: Leaf decomposition and discoloration, ranging from pitting or fungal infestation (top) through miner larvae (second from top) to complete destruction of the soft leaf tissues (bottom).

Exemplary recycling

Icy fruit instead of fruit ice—the drupes of European cranberry bush

The perpetual cycle—new formation of leaf organs, shedding of dispensable components, and decomposition of those components to the point of reusable mineral recycling—is repeated afresh each year. Nature shows us how to keep the majority of the nutrients on site, with no significant loss of substance, and thus how to manage things economically on a long-term basis.

Only in recent times have acid rain and the related changes in the environment greatly disturbed the pH and natural buffering of the soils and caused sizable problems.

In the photo: With some species, the ripe fruits have to become thoroughly and solidly frozen before animals can eat them. As frozen food, they stay on the boughs far into winter.

Alpine dwarf shrub heath above the timberline.

Identifying Shrubs

Shrubs are a great deal more than a wild tangle of branches or an impenetrable thicket. Native and imported species present themselves in different guises all year long—in winter their bark and bud structures are especially prominent; from spring into late summer they are showily arrayed in blossoms; and in fall they display ripe fruits or brilliantly colored foliage. The bulk of the year, the deciduous shrubs bear leaves. They can be easily and accurately identified by means of characteristic features of their leaves.

Advice and Tips on Identification

Barron's Color-key System As an Aid to Identification

The leaves of wild and ornamental shrubs can be assigned to morphological groups that are easily visible at a glance, on the basis of features of leaf blade division, leaf margin configuration, and leaf arrangement.

Yellow bar: On pages 62 to 127 you will find shrubs with single, smooth-margined leaves. However, also arranged in this section are those species whose margins are so finely dentate or crenate that they appear almost smooth unless viewed under a magnifying glass.

Green bar: On pages 128 to 165 you will find shrubs with dentate, serrate, crenate, or lobed leaves.

Blue bar: On pages 166 to 193 you will find all the shrub species with compound (pinnate) leaves, independently of whether the leaf margin is dentate, crenate, or lobed.

Lilac bar: On pages 194 to 207 you will find shrubs with needlelike (acicular) or scalelike leaves. Brought together here are all the species that are affiliated with the gymnosperms, such as common juniper and savin juniper, as well as a number of angiosperms, like heather or tamarisk, that have reduced their leaves to a needle or scale format.

How the Species Were Chosen

In this Barron's nature guide, you will find all the important and interesting wild shrubs of Central Europe as well as neighboring regions as far as the southern edge of the Alps. In addition, it includes a large number of ornamental shrubs whose home is predominantly the portions of North America or East Asia with a comparable climate. Excluded for the most part were small species from very difficult groups that cannot be clearly summed up (such as the shrub willows and their hybrids, many wild roses, or the small species of the native blackberry). Where the introduced or naturalized ornamental shrubs are concerned, it is usually the wild form that is presented.

The Profiles

All the color photos were taken in the open countryside. They show the shrub species with their characteristic leaf and growth features, frequently during blooming season or adorned with fruits. In the course of growing and developing, blooming and ripening, and also depending on the specific habitat, the plants change their appearance to a certain extent. The photographs, which are candid shots, cannot capture all the details of this process of growth, change, and decay. **The descriptions** contain concise, easy-to-follow,

Explanatory notes on the identification section

yet accurate information that is essential for quick identification of the species.

Plant names: Listed here are both the common English name and the scientific or botanical name in keeping with the most recent information published in European floras. Also included is the plant family to which the species in question belongs. Within the four color-key groups, the species are arranged according to their leaf characteristics and their family affiliation, and they appear in alphabetical order according to the scientific name of their genus.

Every profile contains the following information:

Appearance: The shrub's outward appearance, size, and overall impression at first glance. **Stems and branches** have a profound effect on the outward appearance of the plant. The necessary particulars appear under this heading. **The leaves,** as long-lived organs, are particularly important for recognition outside the blooming season. Special pointers make the characteristic features of the leaf shape and leaf arrangement easier to understand. Because **flowers** also provide important identifying features, as many details as possible of their color, form, and

size are given here, along with comments on the structure of their inflorescence. Insofar as the **fruits** are particularly conspicuous, they also are described briefly.

Blooming season: The data on the blooming season apply to the Central European area of the respective species and to their habitat. North American seasons will be similar—a little earlier in somewhat warmer areas and later in somewhat colder areas.

Occurrence: Habitat and biological community in which the species concerned appears naturally. Alternatively, its use as an ornamental woody plant.

Identification tip: Here, reliable identifying and distinguishing features are given for similar species. Closely related species that otherwise are not treated in detail are also presented under this heading.

Gardening tip: Notes on the ecological significance of the species concerned as far as native wildlife is concerned. Also, notes on planting and care in parks and gardens.

The Silhouettes
As a supplement to the colored bars, you will find the following silhouettes:

Smooth-margined opposite simple leaves

Smooth-margined alternate simple leaves

Serrate, dentate, crenate, or lobed opposite simple leaves

Serrate, dentate, crenate, or lobed alternate simple leaves

Opposite compound (pinnate) leaves

Alternate compound (pinnate) leaves

Needlelike or scale-like leaves

Nature Conservation
Some native wild shrubs are specially protected under the Endangered Species Act. Because of their scarcity, they may not be harmed, or worse, dug up. Please remember that cutting brushwood from native wild shrubs for purposes of decoration is not a good practice and may even be prohibited in some areas.

Simple, Smooth-Margined Leaves

Leaves with a largely smooth margin that looks as if it had been cut out with scissors exemplify this leaf type: the simple foliage leaf. Although their basic design is quite plain and simple, they nonetheless manage to produce an abundance of shapes.

The outward appearance of a smooth-margined simple foliage leaf also includes special features: the petiole length, any stipules that may be present, the nature of the leaf surface, and the number and course of the leaf veins. Each combination of individual characteristics is usually so distinctive that the separate species of shrubs can be accurately identified on the basis of the major leaf features alone.

European fly honeysuckle is a very attractive and ecologically valuable shrub, especially when adorned with fruit.

The nectar-bearing flowers . . .

attract a great many lepidoptera

Butterfly bush

Butterfly Bush, Summer Lilac
Buddleja davidii
Buddlejaceae

Appearance: Medium-sized deciduous shrub, when free-standing becomes very broad, dense, and bushy, singly or in fairly small groups, up to about 10' (3 m). Leaves penniveined, elliptic to lance-olate, opposite, 2" to 10" (6–25 cm) long and 1" to 3" (2–7 cm) wide, dentate, upper surfaces dull green, undersides gray or white and fuzzy. Branches twiggy and very long, slightly arching. Young growth hairy. Flowers four-lobed, with narrow corolla tube, bright yellow near the tube opening, otherwise (depending on the cultivar) blue-violet or reddish, rarely also pure white. Numerous single flowers arranged in upright, spikelike terminal panicles. Capsular fruits inconspicuous.

Blooming season: July–August. Fruit ripening in September.

Occurrence: Originally only in East Asia (China and Japan), where it grows in bottom land along bodies of running water and in thickets on rocky ground. Frequently cultivated and also found growing wild in waste places or along railroads.

Identification tip: The long-acuminate leaves and lush inflorescences cannot be confused with any other ornamental shrub.

Gardening tip: Tolerates little shade. Decidedly attractive to butterflies, during blooming season visited primarily by diurnal lepidoptera (red admiral, peacock butterfly, painted lady). Can freeze back fairly hard in winter, but continues to put forth again.

Cornaceae

Tatarian dogwood

Cornelian cherry in flower

Cornus species are equally attractive whether bearing flowers or fruits. Only the inviting drupes of cornelian cherry are edible. For birds and small mammals, the fruits of all the Cornus species are a valuable supply of additional food.

Cornelian cherry, fruits

Tatarian Dogwood, Red-barked Dogwood
Cornus alba
Cornaceae

Appearance: Densely leaved deciduous ornamental shrub, not stoloniferous, up to 10' (3 m). Leaves with arching veins, elliptic-oval, upper surfaces bright green, undersides bluish. Flowers small, yellowish white, numerous, in corymbs 1" to 2" (3–5 cm) across. Drupes light blue or whitish, inedible.
Blooming season: May–June. Fruit ripening in July.
Occurrence: Indigenous to East Asia from Siberia to North Korea.
Identification tip: The coral-red bark of most cultivars is unmistakable.
Gardening tip: Tolerates little shade. Notable for early leaf production and beautiful fall foliage. The drupes are a valuable food for songbirds. Numerous cultivars are in use.

Cornelian Cherry, Cornel
Cornus mas
Cornaceae

Appearance: Deciduous shrub or small tree with spreading branches, up to about 26' (8 m). Leaves are the same color on both sides, upper surfaces shiny. Flowers produced before leaves, light yellow, borne in small umbels. Drupes hanging, bright red. Edible.
Blooming season: February–April. Fruit ripening in July.
Occurrence: Woods edges, margins, meadowland hedges, thickets.
Identification tip: Early blooming date, leaves usually have three to four arching veins.
Gardening tip: Suitable for mixed hedges. Valuable wild fruit bush; favored by birds. Often part of the roadside vegetation.

Red dogwood, flowers

Swedish dogwood, flowers

Swedish dogwood, fruits

Red dogwood, fruits

Red Dogwood
Cornus sanguinea
Cornaceae
Appearance: Deciduous shrub or tree, up to 16½' (5 m). Leaves elliptic, acuminate, short-stalked, with three pairs of arching veins. Flowers pure white, in dense corymbs, appearing after the leaves. Drupes globular, inedible.
Blooming season: May–June. Fruit ripening in September.
Occurrence: Meadowland hedges, thickets in bottom land, deciduous forests, roadside vegetation, on stony soils.

Identification tip: Sunny side of stem bark (especially in winter) is dark red. Flowers have fishy odor.
Gardening tip: Valuable woody plant for hedges, also provides shelter for birds. Produces runners; has splendid fall foliage.

Swedish Dogwood
Cornus suecica
Cornaceae
Appearance: Small in stature, forming very little wood at the base, and usually herbaceous, up to about 10" (25 cm). Leaves broad-elliptic, with arching venation.

Branches four-sided, mostly dark red, prostrate or ascending. Flowers white, in small umbelliform heads. Drupes red, inedible.
Blooming season: May. Fruit ripening in July.
Occurrence: Bogs, dwarf shrub communities on acid soils.
Identification tip: Procumbent, herbaceous stems and very large floral envelope.
Gardening tip: Very good as underplanting for shrubs or hedges. The very similar **Canadian dogwood** (*Cornus canadensis*) is more frequently available commercially.

Celastraceae

Common spindle tree, flowers

Common spindle tree in fruit

Common spindle tree, fruits (poisonous!)

Common Spindle Tree, European Euonymus, Spindleberry

Euonymus europaea
Celastraceae

Appearance: Deciduous shrub or small tree, singly or in a stand, branches dense and wide-spreading, 6½' to 20' (2–6 m). Leaves alternate, oval-lanceolate and acuminate, short-stalked, upper surfaces dark green, undersides slightly bluish, largely smooth-margined or at most inconspicuously crenate, in fall turning coppery red. Branches tough and strong, wood yellowish, previously made into charcoal for drawing and into various kinds of turned pieces (spindles). Flowers inconspicuous, tetramerous, greenish, long-stalked, borne in the leaf axils, only slightly fragrant. Capsular fruits with four valves, crimson when ripe. The seeds are quite large and whitish, but in the capsule they are surrounded by a highly contrasting orange-red seedcoat. **Very poisonous!**

Blooming season: May–June. Fruit ripening in September.

Occurrence: Stands of woody plants in fields, thickets, edges of woods and paths.

Identification tip: The stems and branches are smooth, green, and four-edged. The annual shoots are lined with edge-reinforcing corky ridges at the base.

Gardening tip: Also tolerates shade. Decorative and valuable woody plant favored by birds (nesting area, food, cover), deserves to be used more frequently despite having parts that are poisonous to humans. Often planted as an ornamental because of its showy, usually very abundant decorative fruits. Prefers nitrogen-rich, moderately warm locations.

Celastraceae

Broad-leaved spindle tree, fruits

Warty spindle tree, flowers

Broad-leaved spindle tree, flower

Spindle tree, corky ridges

While birds consume the seeds and fruits of the Celastraceae without harm, all the species of this genus are extremely poisonous for humans. They contain substances that affect the heart, very similar to those in foxglove.

Broad-leaved Spindle Tree

Euonymus latifolia
Celastraceae
Appearance: Deciduous, small to medium-sized wild shrub with erect, wide-spreading branches, up to 16½' (5 m). Leaves oblong-oval, finely acuminate, up to 5" (12 cm) long. Flowers mostly pentamerous, petals greenish, red at the edges. Fruit capsule has five valves, squared with narrow winged border. Seeds white, with orange-red seedcover. **Very poisonous!**
Blooming season:
May–June. Fruit ripening in September.
Occurrence: Herb-rich mixed forests in mountainous areas.
Identification tip: Pentamerous flowers, rounded branches, and leafstalks with grooved channeling distinguish it from the common spindle tree.
Gardening tip: Thus far, little used as an ornamental shrub, but a valuable species for natural gardens.

Warty Spindle Tree

Euonymus verrucosa
Celastraceae
Appearance: Small deciduous shrub with spreading stems, up to 6½' (2 m). Leaves oval-lanceolate. Flowers greenish, with dark red dots. Yellow-red capsular fruits. Seeds black, covered by blood-red seedcover. **Poisonous!**
Blooming season:
May–June. Fruit ripening in September.
Occurrence: Eastern and southeastern Europe from Poland and Austria to the Urals.
Identification tip: Branches and stems have large numbers of black-brown warts.
Gardening tip: Rarely used as an ornamental shrub, but valuable for natural gardens.

Tutsan hypericum, flowers and fruits

Hypericum

Leaf arrangement

The flowers of the Guttiferae yield copious amounts of nectar.

Tutsan Hypericum
Hypericum androsaemum
Guttiferae
Appearance: Densely branched evergreen shrub with creeping or ascending stems, 12" to 32" (30–80 cm). Leaves sessile, hairless, up to 4" (10 cm) long and 2½" (6 cm) wide, obtuse-ovate, leathery, dotted with translucent oil glands. Flowers light yellow, up to about 1" (3 cm) wide, long-stalked. Berries initially red-brown, turning shiny black, inedible.
Blooming season: June–August. Fruit ripening in August.

Occurrence: Woods and thickets in parts of western and southern Europe where winters are mild.
Identification tip: The large, leathery leaves, blue-green underneath, are characteristic.
Gardening tip: Rarely planted as an ornamental, but highly recommended for natural gardens.

Hypericum, St.-John's-wort, Aaron's Beard
Hypericum calycinum
Guttiferae
Appearance: Densely branched, bushy evergreen shrub with large numbers of stolons, 8" to 24" (20–60 cm). Leaves short-stalked, obtuse-elliptic, with translucent dots. Flowers up to 3" (7 cm) wide, solitary, long-stalked. Capsular fruits brown-red, hanging.
Blooming season: July–September.
Occurrence: Thin woods, stony escarpments.
Identification tip: Smooth capsular fruit, stems squared and lined with two narrow ridges.
Gardening tip: Tolerates shade and is frequently used as a ground cover. Of minor value to our native wildlife.

Slender deutzia, stand

Deutzias have long been grown for ornamental use, in a great many species and cultivars. They are extremely attractive, particularly during the blooming season. They are of minor significance for native wildlife.

Slender deutzia, flowers

Slender Deutzia, Japanese Snow Flower
Deutzia gracilis
Hydrangeaceae

Appearance: Rather bushy, rampant, deciduous ornamental shrub, with arching, slightly squared, hollow branches, about 3' (1 m). Leaves decussate, oblong-oval, wedge-shaped at the base, long-acuminate, 1" to 3" (3–7 cm) long, upper surfaces distinctly downy, undersides only slightly downy, penniveined. Flowers borne in large numbers, in erect panicles at the ends of shoots having leaves, pentamerous, white petals outspread in star shape, narrow-oval. Capsular fruits inconspicuous.

Blooming season: May–June.
Occurrence: Native to East Asia (Japan).

Identification tip: Many other species of this genus, which is of largely Asiatic origin, are commercially available in various cultivars, including some with pink or double flowers. **Fuzzy deutzia** *(Deutzia scabra)* has especially prominent stellate hairs on its leaves and produces white or reddish flowers up to 1" (3 cm) across. In **long-leaved deutzia** *(Deutzia longifolia)*, the narrow lance-olate leaves look bluish-green and are covered with many-rayed stellate hairs. The outsides of the flowers are pink to purple in color.

Gardening tip: Several cultivars frequently are used as ornamentals. *Deutzia* species (hybrids) tolerate semishade and are fairly hardy even in our climate. Only hard freezes are not well tolerated.

Buxaceae

Common box in its habitat

Common box, inflorescences

Common box is one of the few evergreen broad-leaved trees native to Central Europe. Although it is particularly widespread south of the Alps, it also tolerates moderately harsh winters and for this reason is a traditional component of small formal hedges.

Common Box, Boxwood
Buxus sempervirens
Buxaceae
Appearance: Densely branching evergreen wild shrub or small tree with erect stems and branches, up to 23' (7 m). Bark conspicuously smooth, brown, only in very old specimens breaking into longitudinally cracked patches or strips in the trunk area. Leaves opposite, short-stalked, oval to rounded, obtuse or slightly emarginate, glossy dark green on upper side, light green on under-side, leathery and firm. Flowers small, inconspicuous, yellowish. Brownish capsular fruits inconspicuous. **All parts of the plant are mildly poisonous!**
Blooming season: March–April.
Occurrence: Prefers sunny slopes, thickets on rocks, or open woods on stony, for short periods also very dry, soil. In warm regions (vine-growing regions) from Central Europe (northernmost wild occurrence on the lower Moselle) to the Near East.
Identification tip: The evergreen, rather crowded leaves are typical.
Gardening tip: Very fre-quently cultivated in parks and gardens as decorative, firm woody plant. Box is an old plant traditionally found in monastery and convent gardens and in country gardens. In earlier times it was trained into the shape of very low clipped hedges for use as an edging. Through clipping, especially in French garden architecture, it was also made to take on all kinds of fanciful shapes (topiary work). The flowers have a plentiful flow of nectar. Valuable in hedges or as a solitary plant, also as a nesting place for birds.

Unripe fruits

Ripe fruits

Common privet, flowers

Oval-leaved privet, topiary

Common Privet, European Privet

Ligustrum vulgare
Oleaceae

Appearance: Deciduous and in some cases semi-evergreen wild and ornamental shrub, up to 10' (3 m) or more (16½'–23' [5–7 m]). Leaves short-stalked, somewhat leathery, upper surfaces dark green, undersides lighter, with strong midrib. Branches twiggy, thin, flexible. Flowers tetramerous, in loose panicles, limb of corolla longer than tube, white, very fragrant. Drupes shiny black and inedible.

Blooming season: June–July. Fruit ripening in August.
Occurrence: Meadowland hedges, forest borders. Frequently cultivated.
Identification tip: Loose panicle of flowers and narrow-elliptic, acuminate, dull green leaves.
Gardening tip: Can be pruned, tolerates shade well.

Oval-leaved Privet, Hedging Privet, California Privet

Ligustrum ovalifolium
Oleaceae

Appearance: Semi-evergreen ornamental shrub, usually becoming very compact through pruning, about 3' to 10' (1–3 m) tall. Leaves ovate-elliptic, upper surfaces glossy dark green, undersides yellow-green, hairless on both sides. Flowers creamy white, corolla tube about three times as long as the limb, in dense terminal panicles up to 4" (10 cm) long.
Blooming season: June–July. Fruit ripening in August.
Occurrence: Native to East Asia (Japan, Korea).
Identification tip: Corolla narrower than that of our native privet.
Gardening tip: Ornamental woody plant.

Unripe capsular fruits

White-flowering form

Lilac is a woody plant in transition from a large shrub to a tree. The fragrant flowers are visited by very few insects.

Common lilac, violet-flowering form

Common Lilac, French Lilac

Syringa vulgaris
Oleaceae

Appearance: Large deciduous shrub or tree with rounded crown, 6½' to 20' (2–6 m), rarely to 33' (10 m). Leaves broad-oval, long-acuminate, cordate at base, stalked, 2½" to 5" (6–12 cm) long, both sides the same color and hairless. Venation finely translucent. Branches rounded with gray or brownish-green, smooth bark, on older main stems and on the trunk forming gray, longitudinal fissures. The reddish-brown wood is fairly hard. Flowers with funnel-shaped corolla having four-lobed spreading limb and very narrow tube, shorter than the stamens, blue, violet, reddish, or white; borne in large numbers in dense terminal panicles, strongly and pleasantly scented. Capsular fruits with two valves, brownish.

Blooming season: April–May. Fruits ripening in September.

Occurrence: Native to open woods and thickets in southeastern Europe and the Near East. Growing wild and naturalized on sunny, rocky slopes, along railroad embankments, and on fallow land.

Identification tip: The firm, smooth-margined leaves and the large inflorescences are unmistakable.

Gardening tip: Known in Central Europe since 1560; since that time very popular, commonly used ornamental woody plant. Lilac has to be cut back regularly if it is to retain its shrubby shape. The flowers, so invitingly scented, can be exploited only by especially long-snouted insects. Also of minor ecological significance for other native wildlife.

73

Alpine honeysuckle, flowers

Alpine honeysuckle, fruits (poisonous!)

Blue honeysuckle, fruits (poisonous!)

Alpine Honeysuckle
Lonicera alpigena
Caprifoliaceae
Appearance: Erect deciduous shrub, usually growing singly, about 3' to 10' (1–3 m). Leaves stalked, acuminate. Flowers always in pairs. Double berries globular, glossy bright red. **Poisonous!**
Blooming season: May–July. Fruit ripening in August.
Occurrence: Herb-rich mixed forests in mountains, along margins and paths, in vegetation of tall perennial herbs and timber areas on lime-rich soils. Mountains of Central and southern Europe.

Identification tip: The yellowish-dull red corollas with their labiate structure are especially characteristic.
Gardening tip: Recommended for natural gardens.

Blue Honeysuckle
Lonicera caerulea
Caprifoliaceae
Appearance: Small, but profusely branching deciduous wild shrub, about 3' to 6½' (1–2 m). Leaves short-stalked, rounded oval, initially hairy, later becoming hairless. Flowers in pairs, yellowish-white, with funnel-shaped, almost radial corolla.

Double berries elliptic, black, but with bluish frostlike bloom. **Poisonous!**
Blooming season: April–June. Fruit ripening in July.
Occurrence: Mixed forests and coniferous forests in mountains, alder thickets, and mountain-pine associations on acid, virgin humus soils. European mountain ranges (excluding the Black Forest and the Vosges).
Identification tip: Leaf shape and flower shape clearly differ from those of the previous species.
Gardening tip: Recommended for natural gardens.

Black honeysuckle, fruits (poisonous!)

Boxleaf honeysuckle, fruits (poisonous!)

Black honeysuckle, flowers

Honeysuckles are shrubs that produce strange double flowers and double berries. All the species of this genus have poisonous fruits.

Black Honeysuckle
Lonicera nigra
Caprifoliaceae
Appearance: Fairly small deciduous wild shrub with thin, curved branches, about 3' to 6½' (1–2 m), usually growing singly. Leaves short-stalked, narrow oval to elliptic. Flowers in pairs on long stalks, corolla light pink. Double berries globular, often of unequal size, black, with bluish frostlike bloom. **Poisonous!**
Blooming season:
April–June. Fruit ripening in July.
Occurrence: Woods edges,

path borders, and thickets, especially in the mountains of Central and southern Europe.
Identification tip: The blackish, many-scaled, and relatively small winter buds are especially characteristic.
Gardening tip: Not used as an ornamental woody plant; recommended for natural gardens.

Boxleaf Honeysuckle, Poor Man's Box
Lonicera nitida
Caprifoliaceae
Appearance: Very densely branching evergreen shrub, about 3' to 6½' (1–2 m).

Leaves oblong-oval, about ½" (1 cm) long, upper surfaces glossy dark green. Flowers creamy white, borne in short-stalked pairs on lateral shoots. Double berries shiny purple, pea-sized. **Poisonous!**
Blooming season: May. Fruit ripening in June.
Occurrence: Native to western China.
Identification tip: Branches are decussate, leaves are strikingly small.
Gardening tip: Several cultivars used as ornamental plants, can tolerate moderate shade.

Woodbine honeysuckle, inflorescence

Woodbine honeysuckle in its habitat

Woodbine honeysuckle, fruits (poisonous!)

Woodbine honeysuckle produces long corolla tubes. Only long-snouted butterflies can take advantage of the nectar supplies.

Woodbine Honeysuckle
Lonicera periclymenum
Caprifoliaceae
Appearance: Right-handed deciduous twining shrub, profusely branched and rather densely leaved, 13' to 16½' (4–5 m). Leaves sessile, acuminate or slightly rounded, oblong-oval, hairless, upper surfaces dark green, undersides bluish. Flowers two-lobed, borne in clusters in terminal umbels, with slender, slightly tapering corolla tube up to 2" long, tinged with red before opening, yellow after opening, after pollination even brighter in color; especially toward evening visited and pollinated chiefly by long-snouted moths (hawkmoth species). Double berries globular, often unequal in size, beet-red, shiny. **Mildly poisonous!**
Blooming season: May–August. Fruit ripening in August.
Occurrence: Hedges, thicket borders, woods edges, vegetation in lumber areas, heathland. Fairly common and very widespread in Europe from southern Scandinavia to the Mediterranean region.
Identification tip: The opposite leaves are not fused as in the similar true honeysuckle.
Gardening tip: If you provide stabilizing supports, you can use this profusely flowering, interesting wild shrub to cover walls or high fences. An important source of shelter for birds (nesting area, food supply, cover), also of significance for insects and small mammals.

Caprifoliaceae

Tatarian honeysuckle in flower

The two honeysuckle species pictured here, whose berries are poisonous for humans, are planted rather frequently along streets. They are very decorative, particularly when in fruit in late summer.

European fly honeysuckle, fruits (poisonous!)

Tatarian Honeysuckle
Lonicera tatarica
Caprifoliaceae
Appearance: Erect, rather heavily branching deciduous ornamental shrub, 6½' to 13' (2–4 m). Leaves obtuse-oval, cordate at base. Flowers borne in pairs, corolla light red or white, often striped, split into lobes. Double berries glossy blood-red. **Poisonous!**
Blooming season: May–June.
Occurrence: Native to Eastern Europe and western Asia. Frequently used as ornamental woody plant.
Identification tip: The leaves are hairless.

Gardening tip: Ecologically just as valuable as European fly honeysuckle. Shelters birds.

European Fly Honeysuckle
Lonicera xylosteum
Caprifoliaceae
Appearance: Medium-sized, branching, deciduous wild shrub, about 3' to 10' (1–3 m). Leaves stalked, oval, with a few soft hairs on both sides, ciliate on the margins. Flowers borne in pairs in the leaf axils, with two-lobed, whitish corolla and short, somewhat swollen corolla tube. Double berries pea-sized, dark red, shiny, very juicy. **Mildly poisonous!**
Blooming season: May–June. Fruit ripening in July.
Occurrence: Deciduous and mixed coniferous forests with herbaceous undergrowth, timber areas, thickets. Does not occur in northern Europe.
Identification tip: Leaves hairy, not cordate at base.
Gardening tip: Highly recommended for solitary and hedge plantings in garden use. Valuable shelter for birds, especially songbirds.

Perfoliate honeysuckle, fruits (poisonous!)

Perfoliate honeysuckle in fruit

The honeysuckle species are twining plants that climb with great ease, although you do need to provide them with a supporting surface. The enticing fruits, which appear to be presented on a green serving platter, are poisonous.

Perfoliate Honeysuckle
Lonicera caprifolium
Caprifoliaceae
Appearance: Deciduous right-hand twining shrub, often climbs over 16½' (5 m) high. Leaves decussate, very short-stalked or sessile, elliptic to broad-oval, up to 2" (5 cm) across and twice as long, obtuse at the tip, upper surfaces matte dark green, undersides lighter and bluish. The upper opposite leaves are fused together in pairs. The uppermost leaf pair at the end of the twig forms an elliptic plate. Flowers pentamerous, with very small calyx and 1" (3 cm) funnel-shaped corolla tube whose parted limb doubles back to form two lobes, creamy white, sometimes also tinged with red. Berries rounded or elliptic, beet-red. **Poisonous!**

Blooming season: May–July. Fruit ripening in August.

Occurrence: Open woods and thickets on sunny slopes. Originally only from southeastern Europe to Black Sea region. Very often cultivated in North America and found locally naturalized.

Identification tip: The unusual, fused leaf pairs are especially characteristic.

Gardening tip: Other twining and very enthusiastically climbing ornamental woody plants include the evergreen *Lonicera japonica,* with white-yellow flowers, and *Lonicera henryi,* with purple-red flowers, both of East Asian origin.
Valuable nectar sources and nesting sites.

Caprifoliaceae

Coralberry, flowers

Common snowberry, fruits (poisonous!)

Snowberries have become naturalized in many park grounds. The pure white, poisonous fruits remain on the branches for some time after the leaves have fallen, until they are harvested by birds.

Common Snowberry
Symphoricarpos rivularis
Caprifoliaceae
Appearance: Very profusely stemmed and bushy deciduous ornamental shrub, about 3' to 6½' (1–2 m). Branches fairly thin, faintly squared, pithy or hollow, arching. Leaves short-stalked, rounded-elliptic, upper surfaces dark green, undersides lighter bluish green, hairless or sparsely hairy on the undersides only. Flowers very small, with bell-shaped whitish or reddish corolla, borne in groups in axillary or terminal spikes. Berrylike

drupes with very spongy fruit pulp, globular, variable in size, white. Often persisting even during winter. **Thought to be poisonous!**
Blooming season: June–July. Fruit ripening in September.
Occurrence: Native to Pacific North America, where it is found in the border of coniferous forests on hills and slopes or in woody species in wooded meadows. Introduced to Europe at the beginning of this century and very commonly used as an ornamental shrub in parks. In some places escaped and naturalized.

Identification tip: Coralberry or **Indian currant** (*Symphoricarpos orbiculatus*) is similar in many respects. Its globular to elliptic inedible drupes are reddish to crimson. It also comes from North America and in recent years has been planted with increasing frequency in parks and gardens.
Gardening tip: Low-growing cultivars of snowberry (including hybrids crossed with coralberry) are planted as ground covers.

Rhamnaceae

Alpine buckthorn, fruits (poisonous!)

Alpine buckthorn in flower

Common buckthorn of Europe, fruits (poisonous!)

Alpine Buckthorn
Rhamnus alpina
Rhamnaceae
Appearance: Usually slender, unarmed deciduous wild shrub, about 3' to 10' (1–3 m) tall. Leaves up to about 5" (12 cm) long, broad oval, rounded at tip, with seven to 20 pairs of lateral veins. Flowers inconspicuous, greenish yellow, borne in bunches in the leaf axils, dioecious. Drupes blue-black, seeds shiny yellow. **Poisonous!**
Blooming season: May–July. Fruit ripening in July.
Occurrence: Forest borders, thickets along bodies of running water, and rocky slopes in the mountains of southern Europe to the Pyrenees.
Identification tip: The large numbers of only slightly arching leaf veins are striking.
Gardening tip: Recommended for natural gardens.

Common Buckthorn of Europe
Rhamnus cathartica
Rhamnaceae
Appearance: Medium-sized deciduous wild shrub with spines, somewhat wide-spreading branches, to 10' (3 m), or small tree to about 26' (8 m). Leaves with short point, very finely serrate, with three to four lateral veins. Flowers tetramerous, inconspicuous, greenish, borne in the leaf axils. Drupes black with dull luster. **Poisonous!**
Blooming season: April–June. Fruit ripening in September.
Occurrence: Margins, woody species in meadows, thickets, meadowland hedges.
Identification tip: The lateral veins of the leaves are strongly arched.
Gardening tip: Useful for wild hedges and plantings that shelter birds.

Dwarf buckthorn, flowers

Dwarf buckthorn, fruits (poisonous!)

Rock buckthorn, fruits (poisonous!)

Dwarf Buckthorn
Rhamnus pumila
Rhamnaceae
Appearance: Recumbent or creeping, profusely branched, thornless small wild shrub (low-spreading shrub), up to 8" (20 cm). Leaves borne at the twig ends, clustered in tufts, oval. Flowers tetramerous, inconspicuous greenish-yellow, bisexual or unisexual. Drupes globular, blue-black, with dull luster. **Poisonous!**
Blooming season: May–July. Fruit ripening in July.
Occurrence: Pioneer colonizers and rock-dwellers, paricularly on limy rocks at the alpine altitude line up to 7710' (2350 m), in the high mountains of Central and southern Europe. Cultivated in North America.
Identification tip: The short-stalked oval leaves and the gnarled branches are characteristic.
Gardening tip: Suitable for natural gardens.

Rock Buckthorn
Rhamnus saxatilis
Rhamnaceae
Appearance: Usually relatively small deciduous wild shrub with spines and wide-spreading branches, up to 6½' (2 m). Leaves fairly small, elliptic, acuminate, upper surfaces light green with dull luster. Shoots hairy, with brown-red bark. Flowers tetramerous, inconspicuous, light yellow, borne in clusters in the leaf axils. Drupes shiny black. **Poisonous!**
Blooming season: April–May.
Occurrence: Pyrenees to the Balkans. Cultivated in North America.
Identification tip: Leaves noticeably smaller than in the similar common buckthorn of Europe.
Gardening tip: Suitable for natural gardens.

81

European mistletoe in fruit

European mistletoe, seedling

European mistletoe with sticky seeds (poisonous!) roping down

European mistletoe, male flowers

European Mistletoe
Viscum album
Loranthaceae
Appearance: Usually branches quite profusely, spherical evergreen shrub up to about 3' (1 m) in diameter, growing on broad-leaved trees. Leaves about 2" (5 cm) long and up to ½" (1 cm) wide, leathery and coarse, oblong-ligulate, rounded at tip, same yellowish-green on both sides, shed after about 15 months. Flowers dioecious, inconspicuous, borne singly or in groups at the shoot ends. Accessory fruits globular, whitish, consisting of very sticky fruit pulp in which several seeds with an additional episperm are embedded. **Poisonous!**
Blooming season: March–April. Fruit ripening in September of the same year.
Occurrence: Widespread and common in parts of Central and southern Europe with mild winters, from the plains to hilly country; in the mountains, up to about 4266' (1300 m).
Identification tip: These mistletoes grow mostly on deciduous trees, primarily poplars, willows, birches, hornbeams, robinias (locust trees), chestnut trees, and fruit trees (especially apple trees), however, not on beeches or oaks. They are semiparasites, taking only water and minerals from the surface on which they grow, hence the damage done to the carrier tree is usually limited. Only a massive infestation causes problems.
Gardening tip: Mistletoes, which are fascinating from a biological standpoint, can easily be colonized on fruit trees. To do so, spread the ripened seeds on a branch in spring. Germination is a very slow process, however.

Viscum laxum on a conifer

European mistletoe in a stand

Ecologically, mistletoes are extremely interesting plants. Unfortunately, they are increasingly plundered for use as decoration. If the infestation is moderate, they do no harm at all to their host trees. The whitish or yellowish fruits are poisonous!

Mistletoe
Viscum laxum
Loranthaceae
Appearance: Globular ever-green shrub up to about 3' (1 m) in diameter, with a short trunk and regularly forking branches. Leaves spatulate, coarse and leathery, in winter more emphatically yellowish-green than in sum-mer. Flowers dioecious, with-out stalks, borne in groups at the ends of the shoot axes. The globe-shaped accessory fruits turn from greenish to yellowish-white and ripen during the winter months. **Poisonous!**

Blooming season: March–April.
Occurrence: In the natural distribution range of conifer-ous trees, in intermediate and higher mountain ranges throughout Europe.
Identification tip: Some-times these mistletoes, which grow on conifers, are lumped together with the very closely related *V. album* to form a single species. In any event, among the conifer-dwelling forms, two different forms (subspecies) with distinct host-specificity can be distin-guished. Fir-dwelling mistle-toes occupy the silver fir

almost exclusively. Their fruits are oblong-ovate. The pine-dwelling mistletoe pro-duces smaller, yellowish fruits and occurs primarily on the Scotch pine. The Euro-pean larch always remains free of mistletoe; the Japan-ese larch, cultivated by forestry experts, can carry both forms of the conifer-dwelling mistletoe, however.
Gardening tip: Colonization on garden shrubs and trees as for *V. album,* though less likely to succeed.

Apocynaceae

Greater periwinkle, flowers

Common periwinkle in flower

The lobes of periwinkle petals are slanted at the tip, which means that the wheel-shaped flower is no longer strictly radially symmetrical. All the parts of the plant are slightly poisonous!

Greater Periwinkle, Large Periwinkle

Vinca major
Apocynaceae
Appearance: Subshrub with creeping shoot axes that root at the nodes and ascending or overhanging branches. Leaves leathery, lanceolate, up to 3½" (9 cm) long, larger toward the end of the twig. Flowers up to 2" (5 cm) across, light blue to blue-violet, with short tube and wide lobes resembling a mill wheel. Fruits follicular.
Blooming season: March–May (also September–October).
Occurrence: Native to the Mediterranean region, in shady woods and meadows.
Identification tip: Leaves matte green, ciliate on the margins.
Gardening tip: Often used as ground cover. Shade-tolerant, makes good underplanting for hedges.

Common Periwinkle, Lesser Periwinkle

Vinca minor
Apocynaceae
Appearance: Evergreen subshrub with thin, creeping shoot axes. Only flowering branches grow to 8" (20 cm). Leaves short-stalked, leathery, up to 2" (5 cm) long, lanceolate. Flowers blue to blue-violet, corolla tube funnel-shaped, lobes of corolla slanting (mill wheel shape). Fruits follicular.
Blooming season: March–April.
Occurrence: Woods, thickets, hedges, western and southern parts of Central Europe, frequently growing wild and naturalized.
Identification tip: Leaves wedge-shaped at base and not ciliate.
Gardening tip: Shade-tolerant ground cover.

Old English lavender, flowers

Lavender is a particularly treasured aromatic flower. It is almost irresistible to flower-visiting insects (primarily bees and bumblebees) as well. It can have the same effect in flower or herb gardens also.

Field of lavender in southern France (Provence)

Old English Lavender
Lavandula angustifolia
Labiatae
Appearance: Usually profusely stemmed, bushy evergreen wild shrub with ascending, fairly stiff stems that produce squared short shoots, about 3' (1 m) high. Leaves opposite, narrow-lanceolate to linear, up to 2" (5 cm) long, narrowing at both ends, obtuse, not sharp, margins slightly involuted, both sides gray and feltlike, occasionally also hairless. Flowers labiate, short-stalked, with downy gray to bluish calyx and lavender-blue corolla, whose tube is only slightly taller than the calyx, borne in very large numbers in erect, long-stalked, spike-like inflorescences, each consisting of several false whorls. All parts of the plant are pleasantly aromatic.
Blooming season: June–August.
Occurrence: Sunny, dry slopes on stony, shallow soil, primarily in the western Mediterranean region, from flat land up to 5562' (1700 m).
Identification tip: Spike *(Lavandula latifolia)* is quite similar. Its inflorescences are more compact, and the single flowers each possess two gray, downy bracts.
Gardening tip: The hybrid produced by crossing the two species, frequently called lavandin, is cultivated in southern France to obtain its aromatic essence. It also is sold as a garden plant. Lavender is hardy in Central Europe as well. Valuable forage plant for flower-visiting insects. Requires a sunny location in an herb garden or among roses.

85

Hyssop

Hyssop, portion of the inflorescence

Hyssop is a less well-known but highly recommended species for aromatic or herb gardens that are frequented by bees and bumblebees. The lower lip of the splendid labiate flower is very well developed.

Hyssop
Hyssopus officinalis
Labiatae

Appearance: Large herbaceous plant or (in some cases) evergreen subshrub with recumbent or erect stems and squared branches, about 24" (60 cm) tall. Leaves decussate, tufted only on short shoots and hence appearing to be arranged in whorls, sessile, up to 2" (5 cm) long, linear to narrow-lanceolate. Calyx regularly five-toothed with long awn tips, corolla two-lobed, bright blue, rarely also violet, reddish, or pure white. Large numbers of single flowers, arranged in spikelike terminal inflorescences bending to one side, with several many-flowered false whorls. All parts of the plant exude a pleasant, aromatic scent when stripped off or crushed between one's fingers.

Blooming season: July–September.

Occurrence: Native to southern Europe (Mediterranean region), prefers dry, stony, shallow slopes on limy subsoil. Has long been grown in gardens, and in many places has escaped from cultivation and become naturalized throughout eastern North America.

Identification tip: The lower labium of the corolla is clearly larger than the somewhat indistinct upper labium, and the stamens are much taller. The plant has a great diversity of forms and certain of its features, including hairiness and calyx shape, can vary.

Gardening tip: The plant is hardy despite its Mediterranean origin. Highly decorative, valuable forage plant for flower-visiting insects. Medicinal and aromatic plant for herb gardens.

Rosemary, revolute leaf

Rosemary, single flower

Rosemary, old shrub

Rosemary
Rosmarinus officinalis
Labiatae
Appearance: Very densely branching, bushy evergreen shrub with erect or ascending stems, about 3' to 6½' (1–2 m), occasionally also decumbent. Branches with gray bark. Leaves decussate, coarse, leathery, sessile, up to 1½" (4 cm) long, margins involuted, tips rounded, not sharp, upper surfaces dark green with dull luster or slightly wrinkled, undersides covered with white down, and numerous stellate hairs. Flowers pentamerous, two-lobed, with bell-shaped calyx and light-blue, sometimes also violet-blue or whitish corolla, whose tube is taller than the calyx. Upper labium doubly cleft and bent far back. The flowers are combined in small numbers in axillary racemes resembling false whorls and appear primarily on the upper third of the branches. All parts of the plant smell pleasantly aromatic when rubbed between one's fingers.
Blooming season: January–April.
Occurrence: Dry, sunny slopes on limestone rock, open thickets, forest borders. Distinguishing plant of the macchia (maquis) in the Mediterranean region.
Identification tip: Especially distinctive are the stiffly upright stems and branches and the early flowering date.
Gardening tip: In areas that are not above freezing in winter, rosemary can be grown only in pots or tubs, because it is not frost-resistant. Rosemary leaves are an essential ingredient of the herb blend known as "herbes de Provençe."

Common sage, inflorescence

Common sage

Common sage, leaves used for seasoning

Common or Garden Sage
Salvia officinalis
Labiatae

Appearance: Many-stemmed evergreen subshrub with prostrate or downward-bending small trunks and stems, from which ascend largely herbaceous and densely leaved branches, about 20" (50 cm) high. Leaves decussate, mostly semi-evergreen, rather coarse and firm, stalked, smooth-margined or very finely crenate, conspicuously wrinkled, upper surfaces gray-green and covered with dense hairs at first, undersides white and feltlike, depending on the cultivar streaked with dark violet, especially during the cold season. Flowers pentamerous, with rich brown-red, two-lobed calyx and violet-blue corolla up to 1½" (3.5 cm) long, the lower labium being larger than the upper and also turning downward. Flowers in false whorls having few blossoms and combined in a terminal, spikelike inflorescence. All parts of the plant smell pleasantly aromatic when crushed between one's fingers or stripped off.

Blooming season: June–July.

Occurrence: Native to the western Mediterranean region, where it is widespread on stony slopes, on fallow land, and along lanes.

Identification tip: The large flowers and the wrinkled, oblong leaves make misidentification unlikely.

Gardening tip: Cultivated in gardens since ancient times and now commercially available in various cultivars. Should be cut back by about one-third in fall. Healing and aromatic plant for herb gardens.

Common thyme in flower

Common Thyme
Thymus vulgaris
Labiatae
Appearance: Many-stemmed, densely bushy small evergreen shrub with erect or ascending stems and branches, up to 16" (40 cm) high. Leaves decussate, small, with leaf margins turning downward at the sides, upper surfaces gray-green, undersides covered with whitish, velvety hair. Flowers pentamerous, distinctly two-lobed, with short calyx and light reddish or very light violet corolla, in tufts in the leaf axils of new shoots and hence appearing to be clustered in heads at the twig ends. All parts of the plant exude a pleasant, intensely aromatic scent when stripped off or crushed between one's fingers.
Blooming season: May–October.
Occurrence: Native to the Mediterranean region, on stony slopes and rocky heaths with strong sun. Occasionally spreads from aromatic plant gardens.
Identification tip: Can be distinguished from other garden-worthy species like **mother-of-thyme** *(Thymus serpyllum)* or *Thymus pulegioides* by its very woody stems and its extremely involuted leaf blades.
Gardening tip: Since antiquity, highly prized as an aromatic plant and cultivated in gardens. Indispensable in scented and aromatic gardens. Has to be cut back slightly each year to preserve its dense, bushy shape. Valuable forage plant for flower-visiting insects. Needs a sunny location.

Star magnolia in flower

Star magnolia, single flower

Magnolia, cultivar

Despite their enchanting appearance, magnolia flowers are simple in structure. In many ways they are reminiscent of the cones of coniferous trees.

Star Magnolia, Starry Magnolia

Magnolia stellata
Magnoliaceae

Appearance: Large deciduous shrub or fairly small tree with many-stemmed, dome-shaped or broadly tapering crown, about 6½' to 16½' (2–5 m).

Leaves 2" to 7" (6–17 cm) long, ½" to 1" (1–3 cm) wide, short-acuminate or obtuse, wedge-shaped at base, upper surfaces dark green, undersides distinctly lighter, hairless or only sparsely hairy, margins occasionally slightly crenate. The flowers appear in advance of the leaves. The sepals and petals are alike in shape, spatulate, pure white, sometimes showing a slight reddish tinge outside, folded back, up to 4" (10 cm) across. The large flower buds are usually terminal, covered with feltlike hair. Annual shoots covered with silky hair. The fruits (if any develop) remain inconspicuous.

Blooming season: March–April.

Occurrence: Native to East Asia (central Japan).

Identification tip: Especially characteristic are the relatively narrow floral leaves (sepals and petals), which spread out in a star shape.

Gardening tip: Several cultivars in use as garden plants. A light-demanding woody plant, not shade tolerant. The commercially available cultivars are relatively slow-growing. An extremely decorative garden plant, it does not develop a need for a great deal of space even after several years, and for that reason it is especially good as an eye-catching solitary specimen plant.

90

Lauraceae

Bay laurel, young fruits

Bay laurel in flower

Bay laurel (bay), which in its homeland forms forests, is the characteristic plant of evergreen Mediterranean sclerophyllous vegetation. For centuries its leaves have been popular for their aroma.

Bay Laurel, Bay, Poet's Laurel, Sweet Bay

Laurus nobilis
Lauraceae

Appearance: Large evergreen shrub or small tree, usually with quite profuse and bushy branches from the base up, initially with a cone-shaped crown, later becoming increasingly rounded, about 3' to 26' (1–8 m).

Leaves are very leathery and coarse, long-stalked, up to 4" (10 cm) long and about 1½" (4 cm) wide, wedge-shaped at base, margins slightly undulate or indistinctly crenate, upper surfaces shiny dark green, undersides matte light green. Lateral veins in the lower leaf half frequently somewhat reddish, exuding a pleasantly aromatic scent when rubbed between one's fingers. Bay is an old kitchen herb.

Flowers are small, greenish-yellow, in groups in the leaf axils, unisexual (dioecious). Berries globe-shaped, about ½" (1 cm) across, green at first, turning dull glossy black when ripe.

Blooming season: March–May. Fruit ripening in September.

Occurrence: Singly on rocky slopes or as undergrowth in open, mixed stands of woody species. Originally only in the Balkans and in Asia Minor. Major characteristic plant of the Mediterranean evergreen sclerophyllous vegetation.

Identification tip: The stiff leaves, traversed by a strong midrib, are unmistakable.

Gardening tip: Although it does tolerate light frost, bay laurel is not hardy in areas that receive freezing temperatures. For this reason it is cultivated largely as a pot or tub plant and overwintered in a greenhouse.

Leguminosae

Judas tree with single flowers borne on the trunk

Judas Tree, Redbud
Cercis siliquastrum
Leguminosae
Appearance: Fairly large deciduous shrub or small tree, about 13' to 20' (4–6 m), usually multi-trunked. Branches and buds intense red-brown. Leaves alternate, rounded, tips obtuse or slightly emarginate, cordate at base, light gray-green when produced, later turning yellowish green, hairless, undersides lighter in color, in fall aspect intense golden yellow to crimson. Flowers clustered, appearing just before leaves, pentamerous, corolla about 1" (2 cm) long, reddish-rose, top two petals much smaller than the three lower ones.
Pods about 2" to 4" (6–10 cm) long, compressed and narrow-winged on the ventral suture, rich brown-red.
Blooming season: March–April. Fruit ripening in September.
Occurrence: Native to Mediterranean region from the northern Adriatic through the entire Balkan area to the Near East. Original range unclear, because so commonly cultivated as ornamental woody plant.

Identification tip: Judas tree exhibits the unusual phenomenon of flower production directly from the trunk or branches (cauliflory), which otherwise occurs almost exclusively in tropical trees. The bright reddish flowers are borne right on the older stems or even on the trunk.
Gardening tip: Since the sixteenth century also in use as a woody plant for parks and gardens. Light-demanding species for limy soil, hardy only in mild sites. Very decorative.

Serviceberry in flower

Serviceberry, young fruits

Serviceberry, flowers

Serviceberry, ripe fruits

Serviceberry, Juneberry, Shadbush

Amelanchier ovalis
Rosaceae

Appearance: Usually very profusely branching and dense-crowned deciduous wild shrub with thin, long stems, about 3' to 10' (1–3 m). Young shoots with feltlike hair, later glossy olive brown. Leaves long-stalked, broad-ovate, rounded at both ends, upper surfaces matte green and hairless, undersides yellowish and feltlike, later becoming hairless and with only axillary awns.
Flowers in groups in terminal panicles, appearing just before the leaves, pentamerous, with long, very narrow, pure white petals. Pomes covered with blue-black frostlike bloom, mealy, pleasant-tasting, edible.
Blooming season: April–June. Fruit ripening in August.
Occurrence: Thickets on rocky ground, sunny, dry steep slopes, or bordering lawns; fond of limestone, from Central Europe to Asia Minor.
Identification tip: The conspicuously abundant flower production, the hairy leaves, and the small, blackish pomes are very characteristic.

Gardening tip: Valuable woody plant for birds (food and nesting area). Of similar value is *Amelanchier lamarckii*, commonly planted in gardens or along streets, very free-flowering, leaves showing a delicate coppery-red color when produced, turning green gradually, and finally displaying handsome fall colors. The black-red pomes, covered with a bluish frostlike bloom, provide food to songbirds in summer as well.

Japanese flowering quince, flowers

Japanese flowering quince in flower

Japanese flowering quince, fruits

Flowering quinces are planted primarily for their striking abundance of flowers and their flower color—an unusual one in a woody plant.

Japanese Flowering Quince, Japonica
Chaenomeles japonica
Rosaceae

Appearance: Small, usually multi-stemmed, thorny or (more commonly) unarmed deciduous shrub with globe-shaped growth, about 3' (1 m). Leaves stalked, broad-oval, 1" to 2" (3–5 cm) long, tips usually obtuse, serrate with slight crenation or largely smooth-margined, somewhat leathery, upper surfaces glossy dark green, undersides light green, penniveined. Flowers pentamerous, grouped in umbellike racemes at the ends of leaf-bearing twigs, sepals greenish-red, petals brick-red to scarlet, outspread in wheel shape, up to about 1" (3 cm) across. Pomes globular, up to 1½" (4 cm) thick, greenish, with orange dots. Very aromatic, but often fairly sour and thus largely inedible raw, though usable if cooked.

Blooming season: March–April. Fruit ripening in June.

Occurrence: Native to East Asia.

Identification tip: The wild plant is virtually unavailable commercially. Instead, an extremely large assortment of hybrids, produced by crossing with **flowering quince** (*Chaenomeles speciosa*), is offered for sale. Usually they remain low-growing and produce especially large orange to crimson flowers.

Gardening tip: Long used in parks and gardens as an early-blooming ornamental woody plant. Highly decorative, interesting forage plant for bees and bumblebees because of its abundant flowers, also useful as nesting site for birds. Needs a sunny location.

Cotoneaster in fruit

Cotoneaster, flowers

Cotoneaster, fruits

Cotoneaster
Cotoneaster integerrimus
Rosaceae
Appearance: Small, densely branching deciduous wild shrub with erect and spreading branches, up to about 3' (1 m). Shoots covered with feltlike hair.

Leaves in an almost two-rowed arrangement, about twice as long as wide and narrowing at both ends, upper surfaces dark green and hairless, undersides covered with dense white to gray feltlike hair, with clearly discernible leaf venation.

Flowers pentamerous, fairly small, bell-shaped, borne singly or in small numbers in terminal racemes, with pale red corolla. Fruits about the size of a pea, scarlet, rounded, hairless, inedible.

Blooming season: April–May. Fruit ripening in August.

Occurrence: Rocks, stony slopes, dry soils, and hillsides covered with rock debris in sunny positions, often in the border of semidry grassplots. Widespread in Europe, in the Alps up to 6592' (2000 m).

Identification tip: The lanceolate leaves, indistinctly acuminate at the tips and felt-like underneath, are unmistakable, as is the smooth, red-brown bark of the older twigs. When rubbed between one's fingers, the bark smells slightly of marzipan.

Gardening tip: *Cotoneaster integerrimus* yields very nectar-rich flowers and hence is popular with hymenopterous insects. The fruits, bright red when ripe, provide a welcome source of nourishment for berry-eating bird species. Also highly suitable for nesting because of the abundant branches. Needs a sunny location and semishade.

95

Fishbone cotoneaster, stand

Cotoneaster tomentosus, flowers

Fishbone cotoneaster, fruits (poisonous!)

Cotoneaster tomentosus, fruits

Fishbone or Herringbone Cotoneaster, Rockspray

Cotoneaster horizontalis
Rosaceae
Appearance: Deciduous to semi-evergreen ornamental shrub with horizontal branches, almost 2' (0.5 m). Leaves two-rowed, broad-elliptic, upper surfaces dark green, undersides only sparsely hairy. Flowers creamy white, borne in the leaf axils, petals erect. Fruits scarlet, **mildly poisonous!**
Blooming season: May–June. Fruit ripening in August.
Occurrence: Native to East Asia (China).

Identification tip: In the similar-appearing *C. dammeri,* the white petals are outspread.
Gardening tip: Ground cover for sunny to semishady locations.

Downy or Wooly Cotoneaster

Cotoneaster tomentosus
Rosaceae
Appearance: Small deciduous wild shrub with over-hanging and spreading branches, about 3' to 6½' (1–2 m). Leaves short-stalked, oval, undersides white, feltlike. Flowers pen-

tamerous, petals whitish, erect. Fruits about as large as peas, bright red, with dull luster, inedible.
Blooming season: April–May. Fruit ripening in September.
Occurrence: Woods, strips of thicket, shrub-rich mixed deciduous stands in dry, warm sites, primarily in Central and southern Europe; cultivated in North America.
Identification tip: In comparison with *C. horizontalis,* the leaves are broader and more rounded.
Gardening tip: Recommended for natural gardens.

Medlar in fruit

Medlar
Mespilus germanica
Rosaceae

Appearance: Only slightly branching deciduous wild shrub or small tree, about 6½' to 16½' (2–5 m). Stems frequently spiny. Shoot tips of the branches frequently covered with gray, feltlike hair. Leaves slightly undulate or finely crenate, but usually completely smooth-margined, oblong-oval, 3" to 5" (8–12 cm) long and up to 1½" (4 cm) wide, slightly cordate at base, finely wrinkled upper surfaces hairy at first, becoming increasingly hairless, under-sides lighter and usually covered with green down. Brilliant yellow in fall aspect. Flowers pentamerous, always solitary, corolla pure white, up to 2" (5 cm) across, flattened. Pomes hairy, reddish-brown. Edible (especially after frost has had its effect).

Blooming season: May–June. Fruit ripening in September.

Occurrence: The name *Mespilus germanica,* or "German medlar," is misleading. The medlar is native to the Mediterranean region, and it was introduced to Central Europe as a fruit tree before medieval times. It has rarely escaped from previous garden cultivation into the wild. Rarely cultivated in North America, but an interesting addition.

Identification tip: The pome, up to about 1" (3 cm) in size and produced from floral axis tissue, is open-topped and—even when ripe—leaves the five-lobed calyx open to view.

Gardening tip: An interesting fruit tree as far as the history of civilization is concerned. Very suitable for mixed orchards or as solitary specimen plant. Prefers loamy soils.

97

Rosaceae

Cherry laurel in its habitat

Cherry laurel, inflorescence

Cherry laurel, fruits (poisonous!)

The shiny drupes of cherry laurel are poisonous!

Cherry Laurel
Prunus laurocerasus
Rosaceae
Appearance: Evergreen ornamental shrub with erect, well-developed stems and branches, about 3' to 16½' (1–5 m).
The stalked leaves are broad-lanceolate, smooth-margined or at most remotely undulate, upper surfaces glossy dark green, undersides lighter dull green, both sides hairless, leathery and firm, 2" to 6" (5–15 cm) long. Leaf margins frequently slightly recurved or involuted. Midrib very pronounced and well developed. Numerous flowers in erect racemes up to 4" (10 cm) long. Sepals about ⅛" (3 mm) long, pure white, about as long as the receptacle. Drupes globular, pea-sized, black.
Poisonous!
Blooming season: April–May, frequently again in September–October. Fruit ripening in July.
Occurrence: In the under-growth of open broad-leaved woods and thickets on rocky slopes, from southwestern Europe to Asia Minor. Rarely cultivated in temperate North America.
Identification tip: The bay-like leaves are thicker and have less undulate margins than those of bay (bay laurel). The leaves do not smell spicy when crushed between one's fingers, but have an aroma of bitter almond. Moreover, the erect inflorescences and fruit structures are distinctly typical of the species.
Gardening tip: Long in use as an ornamental woody plant. Very decorative when used alone, in rows, or as hedge.
Of minor value for wildlife. Suitable for semishade and shade.

Papilionaceae

German broom in flower

English broom, flowers

Many broom species are plants characteristic of the heathlands in the Atlantic climate region. As wild plants, they are rare.

English Broom, Needle Furze

Genista anglica
Papilionaceae
Appearance: Small deciduous wild shrub with wide-spreading branches heavily covered with spines, up to about 1½' (0.5 m). Leaves short-stalked, lanceolate, blue-green. Flowers bright yellow, grouped in terminal racemes. Pods hairless, rounded, light brown, up to nearly 1" (2 cm) long.
Blooming season: May–July. Fruit ripening in August.
Occurrence: Heaths, bogs, open oak, birch, and pine woods. In Atlantic western and Central Europe.
Identification tip: The stems have long spines, the blue-green leaves are hairless.

German Broom

Genista germanica
Papilionaceae
Appearance: Very spiny deciduous wild shrub, up to about 1½' (0.5 m). Leaves, as well as younger branches, densely covered with spreading hairs, long-ciliate on margins, short-stalked to sessile, narrow-lanceolate, grass-green. Flowers golden yellow, numerous, in loose erect terminal racemes.
Pods black-brown, densely covered with hair, few-seeded.
Blooming season: May–August. Fruit ripening in July.
Occurrence: Unfertile meadows, heaths, open woods, sides of lanes.
Identification tip: Branches have long spines, leaves have spreading hairs.
Gardening tip: Not used as an ornamental, but recommended for natural gardens.

99

Downy broom in flower

Dyer's greenwood in flower

Dyer's greenwood, flowers

Broom species exhibit an effective mechanism for dusting visiting insects all over with pollen grains. As soon as a bee or a bumblebee sits on the flower, the carina immediately folds down and thoroughly powders the guest's ventral side.

Downy Broom, Silky-leaf Woadwaxen
Genista pilosa
Papilionaceae
Appearance: Many-stemmed, densely branching, bushy deciduous wild shrub, with prostrate and ascending stems, up to about 1' (0.3 m). Younger branches squared, covered with appressed hairs, older branches longitudinally striped and knotty.
Leaves sessile, lanceolate-oval, folded along the midrib, dark green. Flowers golden-yellow, about ½" (1 cm) across, borne in small numbers in lateral racemes.

Pods light brown, silky, flattened, straight.
Blooming season: May–August. Fruit ripening in July.
Occurrence: Sunny, dry, warm, lime-poor sites in the border of thickets and woods, in heaths and unfertile meadows.
Identification tip: The stems are always thornless, the undersides of the leaves are covered with dense hairs.
Gardening tip: A mat-forming ornamental shrub for sunny sites.

Dyer's Greenweed, Common Woadwaxen
Genista tinctoria
Papilionaceae
Appearance: Multi-stemmed deciduous wild shrub with twiggy branches, 1' to about 3' (0.3–1 m).
Leaves sessile, lanceolate, with silky hairs. Flowers golden yellow, numerous, in erect slender racemes.
Blooming season: June–July.
Occurrence: Heaths, unfertile meadows, open woods.
Identification tip: Branches deeply furrowed, unarmed.
Gardening tip: Very decorative and of value for insects.

Papilionaceae

Spanish broom in flower

During blooming season, Spanish broom consists almost exclusively of green, twiggy stems. Its leaves were shed prematurely to economize on water.

Winged broom in flower

Winged Broom
Genistella sagittalis
Papilionaceae
Appearance: Thornless, mat-forming deciduous dwarf shrub with creeping stalks, up to 10" (25 cm). Leaves sessile, shed early, rounded-oval. Flowers golden-yellow, numerous, in erect terminal racemes. Pods.
Blooming season: May–July.
Occurrence: Unfertile lawns, dry meadows, along paths and lanes, in open thickets and woods. Central and southern Europe. Rarely cultivated in North America.
Identification tip: Branchlets broadly winged and constricted at the nodes.
Gardening tip: Mat-forming dwarf shrub for sunny sites in regions with sandy soil.

Spanish or Weaver's Broom
Spartium junceum
Papilionaceae
Appearance: Profusely branching, bushy deciduous wild shrub, about 1½' to 10' (0.5–3 m). Stems and branches erect, rushlike, finely ribbed. Leaves sessile, lanceolate, shed early. Flowers bright yellow, very fragrant, borne in long, many-blossomed racemes.
Blooming season: April–August.
Occurrence: Macchia (maquis) and garrigue of the Mediterranean area, dry slopes of Atlantic Western Europe. Usually on limy soils.
Identification tip: The rounded, almost leafless twigs are very free-flowering.
Gardening tip: In regions with mild winters, a good ornamental shrub for limy soils in sunny positions.

Oleaster fruit

Oleaster flowers

The silvery gray-green leaves of the oleasters are covered on both sides with marvelous stellate hairs, which are among the loveliest hair structures in the plant kingdom. They reveal their full splendor principally when viewed under a microscope.

Oleaster, Russian Olive
Elaeagnus angustifolia
Elaeagnaceae

Appearance: Medium-sized to large, spiny deciduous shrub or small tree with dense, wide-spreading branches, about 6½' to 16½' (2–5 m); can be taller, although rarely.

Leaves stalked, narrow-lanceolate, about 1½" to 3" (4–8 cm) long × 1" (2 cm) wide, tips acute, wedge-shaped at the base, upper surfaces gray-green and hairless, undersides silvery gray and densely covered with whitish stellate hairs.

Flowers very small, light yellow, leather-scented, bisexual or unisexual (male), borne singly or in small numbers in the leaf axils on the lower part of the branches. Floral envelope consists only of colored sepals.

Accessory fruits about ½" to 1" (1–2 cm) long, cylindrical, light yellow, mealy, very aromatic, edible.

Blooming season: May–July. Fruit ripening in July.

Occurrence: Native to Central Asia, in the seventeenth century introduced to the Mediterranean area, where it now is common along bodies of running water, on lake shores, on the borders of stands of woody plants, and on stony slopes.

Identification tip: The very narrow leaves with their gray-green upper surfaces and the dense covering of stellate hairs on their undersides (lupine characteristic) are unmistakable features.

Gardening tip: Frequently used as a shrub or small tree for parks. Oleasters tolerate pruning, grow very dense, and make excellent windbreaks. They are very productive forage plants for bees and other hymenopterous insects.

Silverberry

Although silverberry is primarily a decorative woody plant for use in parks, its broad-leaved relatives are popular in some places as undemanding windscreens. Today this plant is widespread in dune regions.

Silverberry fruit

Silverberry
Elaeagnus commutata
Elaeagnaceae
Appearance: Densely branched and very bushy deciduous shrub or small tree with brown branches and runners, about 6½' to 16½' (2–5 m).
Leaves broad-oval, 1½" to 3" (4–8 cm) long × 1" to 1½" (2–4 cm) wide, upper surfaces gray-green, undersides whitish, both sides covered with silvery, sometimes also brownish stellate hairs that are easy to see even without a magnifying glass. Flowers cylindrical, silvery outside,

golden-yellow within, borne singly or in small numbers on short stalks in the leaf axils, fragrant.
Fruits dry, silvery.
Blooming season: May–July. Fruit ripening in August.
Occurrence: Native to North America.
Identification tip: Occasionally one sees other, sometimes quite similar, species with broad leaves, such as *Elaeagnus pungens*, whose branches are far spinier than those of the other species.
Gardening tip: Frequently planted in parks because of its decorative, silvery gray

leaves. In coastal regions, extremely suitable for use in dense windbreak plantings. The flowers are a valuable source of nourishment for bees and bumblebees. The dense branches are used by songbirds in particular for brooding and resting.
Elaeagnus species are quite undemanding and suitable for almost any soil, although they do not thrive in semishade or shade.

Elaeagnaceae

Sea buckthorn in fruit

Male inflorescences

Sea buckthorn with copious fruits

Stellate hairs

Sea Buckthorn

Hippophae rhamnoides
Elaeagnaceae

Appearance: Densely branching, medium-sized deciduous wild shrub, about 6½' to 10' (2–3 m); more rarely, also a tree up to about 20' (6 m). Numerous short shoots are modified into long spines at their tips.
Leaves short-stalked, narrow-lanceolate, up to nearly 3" (7 cm) long but no more than ½" (1 cm) wide, wedge-shaped at base, upper surfaces gray-green, undersides silvery gray, both sides covered with large stellate hairs.

Flowers dioecious, inconspicuous, appearing before the foliage, crowded in great profusion on the previous year's branches.
The large, berrylike fruits, bright orange when ripe, develop in an unusual way—from the calyx—and contain large stone seeds, which are rich in vitamins and edible.
Blooming season:
April–May. Fruit ripening in September.
Occurrence: Gravelly meadow ground along alpine bodies of running water, hillsides covered with fine rock debris, inland and coastal

dunes (brown dunes, dune valleys). Widespread in Europe and the Near East.
Identification tip: Some species that grow in mountainous areas have few spines and are not loosely branched. The coastal buckthorn is more vigorous and very spiny, however.
Gardening tip: Frequently grown for ornamental use or planted along roads and highways.
Valuable wild fruit tree, also provides nesting place and food for birds.
Needs a sunny location and loose soils.

Thymelaeaceae

February daphne, fruits

February daphne, flowers

All parts of daphne are poisonous!

February daphne in its habitat

February Daphne, Mezereon
Daphne mezereum
Thymelaeaceae

Appearance: Only slightly branching deciduous small shrub with rod-shaped, very flexible erect or spreading stems and branches, about 1½' to 3' (0.4–1 m). Leaves crowded in tufts at the ends of the branches but in an alternate arrangement, short-stalked, oblong-lanceolate, long wedge-shaped toward the base, upper surfaces vivid green, undersides uniformly gray-green or bluish. Usually the flowers develop only from lower lateral buds along older stems; they are combined in tufts and appear before the leaves. They have an intense fragrance. The corolla is absent; instead, the sepals alone form the rose-purple or crimson floral envelope. The globular, juicy drupes, coral-red when ripe, are, like all other parts of the plant, **extremely poisonous!**

Blooming season: February–April. Fruit ripening in June.

Occurrence: Prefers shady or semishady thickets and mixed deciduous forests on intermittently moist soils. Common in Europe, especially in the mountains and relatively high secondary chains of mountains. In the Alps, up to 6592' (2000 m).

Identification tip: The features of the flowers, leaves, and fruits are unmistakable.

Gardening tip: A very decorative, although poisonous, woody plant. The flowers provide food for lepidoptera early in the season. The fruits are not dangerous for songbirds. Tolerates semishade.

Spurge laurel in flower

Rose daphne in flower

All the daphne species contain strong poisons in all their parts!

Rose Daphne, Garland Flower
Daphne cneorum
Thymelaeaceae
Appearance: Loosely branching small evergreen shrub, 4" to 12" (10–30 cm). Leaves crowded at the terminals of the branches, sessile, oblong to spatulate, leathery, hairless, undersides bluish. Flowers bright pink, lacking corolla, borne in groups in terminal heads.
Drupes yellow or reddish.
Very poisonous!
Blooming season: April–May. Fruit ripening in August.
Occurrence: Thickets and woods in the Alps and the mountains of southern Europe. Cultivated in North America.
Identification tip: In *Daphne striata*, common in the Alps, the petals have a finely striated pattern.

Spurge Laurel
Daphne laureola
Thymelaeaceae
Appearance: Only slightly branching small evergreen shrub with erect stems, up to about 4' (1.2 m).
Leaves stalked, leathery, lanceolate, acuminate, hairless, upper surfaces dull dark green, undersides yellowish. Flowers yellowish-green, slightly fragrant, borne in clusters in hanging, short-stalked racemes in the upper leaf axils. Drupes blue-black.
Very poisonous!
Blooming season: February–May. Fruit ripening in July.
Occurrence: In southern Europe, in open mixed forests. Cultivated in North America.
Identification tip: Not likely to be confused with other *Daphne* species because of the large leaves.
Gardening tip: Suitable for semishady sites. Valuable source of food for birds.

Alpine rose in its high mountain habitat

Alpine Rose, Rock Rhododendron

Rhododendron ferrugineum
Ericaceae

Appearance: Profusely branching small evergreen shrub with strong, erect stems and branches, up to about 4' (1.3 m).

Leaves crowded at the terminals of the branches, distinctly alternate, up to about 5" (12 cm) long and 1½" (4 cm) wide, oblong-lanceolate, tips acuminate to cuspidate, very leathery, very finely dentate on slightly down-turned margins, upper surfaces glossy dark green and hairless, undersides covered thickly with rust-red scalelike hairs. Not especially long-lived, retained by the shrub for only about two years.

Flowers grouped in short compact terminal racemes. The corolla is deep pink to bright pink, up to about 1" (2 cm) long and equally wide, opened in a funnel shape, and covered with short hairs within. The 10 stamens are shorter than the corolla; at the base they are covered with woolly hair.

Capsules woody, brownish. The extremely light seeds are carried off by the wind.

Blooming season: May–July.
Occurrence: Prefers only acid and silicaceous soils in open thickets and woods of the mountain stage up to 9217' (2800 m). Frequently forms stands.
Identification tip: The typically rust-red leaves are unmistakable. The plant almost never is found together with *Rhododendron hirsutum.*
Gardening tip: Not cultivated in gardens.

107

Ericaceae

Hairy-leaved rhododendron in its habitat

Hairy-leaved rhododendron, flower

Hairy-leaved rhododendron, leaves

Sometimes the fungus *Exobasidium rhododendri* causes conspicuous galls on the leaves of Alpine rose

Hairy-leaved Rhododendron

Rhododendron hirsutum
Ericaceae

Appearance: Densely branching and very bushy-looking evergreen shrub with erect, well-developed stems, about 3' (1 m). The leathery, stalked leaves, somewhat resembling bay leaves, are alternate and crowded at the terminals of the branches. They grow only 1" (3 cm) long and ½" (1.5 cm) wide. The upper surfaces are glossy light green and hairless; the undersides are slightly scaly. The margins, as well as the leafstalks, have long, some-what bristly ciliation. The bell-shaped to funnel-shaped flowers are brilliant light red, up to ½" (1.5 cm) long, and almost equally wide. They are borne in headlike, com-pact racemes at the terminals of the branches. The stamens vary in length and are hairy near the base.

The capsules are oval and woody.

Blooming season: May–July, sometimes also until October.

Occurrence: Native only to the central and eastern Alps, especially on limestone at altitudes between 3937' and 8560' (1200–2600 m), some-times forming stands in the dwarf timber belt and other thickets in the area of the timber line, in lower-lying positions, also in damp ravines.

Identification tip: The pronounced ciliation of the leaf margins is especially characteristic.

Rhododendron ponticum in flower

Rhododendron luteum in flower

Rhododendron luteum, flowers

The nectar of *Rhododendron luteum* is poisonous to Central European insects. Pure honeys derived from these plants can also be hard for humans to digest.

Pontic Azalea, Black Sea Azalea

Rhododendron luteum
Ericaceae

Appearance: Densely branched, bushy, medium-sized deciduous shrub, up to about 13' (4 m), spreading successfully by means of branching roots.
Leaves short-stalked, about 4" (10 cm) long and up to 1½" (4 cm) wide, oblong-lanceolate, tips acute, wedge-shaped at base. The leaf margins have barely discernible dentation and dense ciliation; upper surfaces and principal veins on the under-sides covered with bristly hairs.
The flowers appear before the leaves. They are borne at the terminals of the branches in umbellike, crowded racemes. The corolla, up to 2" (5 cm) across, is funnel-shaped, golden-yellow, and intensely fragrant. The five stamens are taller than the corolla.

Blooming season: May.
Occurrence: Coniferous and bog forests from southeastern Central Europe to the Black Sea region.
Identification tip: The deciduous azaleas are distinguished from the evergreen rhododendrons on the basis of their foliage. *Rhododendron ponticum* is an evergreen species. It produces elliptic leaves up to 6" (15 cm) long and large, five-lobed, violet corollas. Native to the Caucasus, in some places (especially in Western Europe) escaped from garden cultivation and naturalized.
Gardening tip: Both of the species named above are the original forms of an enormous number of hybrids and cultivars. Tolerates semi-shade.

109

Miniature rhododendron in flower

Miniature Rhododendron
Rhodothamnus chamaecistus
Ericaceae

Appearance: Profusely branching, bushy, evergreen dwarf shrub, up to 16" (40 cm) high. The leaves, measuring only ½" × ⅛" (10 × 3 mm), are very short-stalked to sessile, tufted at the terminals of the branches, leathery, acute-oval, glossy dark green on both sides, with bristly hairs on the margins. The flowers are long-stalked, up to about 1" (3 cm) wide, and unusually luxuriant for the size of this dwarf plant. Its corolla is showy light pink with darker streaks and spots, and the lobes of the corolla are spread out in a wheel shape. They are always produced on the previous year's shoots.
Capsules with numerous, very light seeds.

Blooming season: May–July.
Occurrence: Stony slopes, slopes covered with rock debris, and rock crevices in limestone. Eastern Alps (Austria) and Karawanken.
Identification tip: Alpine azalea *(Loiseleuria procumbens)* is closely related. A low-spreading deciduous shrub, it forms extensive, very flat, dense mats. Its leaves are short-stalked, hairless, and glossy dark green. The rose-red, pentamerous flowers measure no more than ½" (1 cm) across and are produced in racemes having few blossoms, at the terminals of the branches. In the Alps above the elfin woodland belt up to 9843' (3000 m) on primitive rock.
Gardening tip: Not suitable for garden cultivation.

Ericaceae

Bog rosemary in flower

Bog Rosemary
Andromeda polifolia
Ericaceae
Appearance: Very sparsely branching evergreen dwarf shrub with far-creeping shoot axis, rooting repeatedly at the nodes, and thin, arching, ascending branches, 8" to 16" (20–40 cm).

Leaves short-stalked, very leathery, usually pointing upward, linear to narrow-lanceolate, narrowed at both ends, with short spiny tip, leaf margins revolute, upper surfaces usually glossy dark green with indented midrib and hairless, undersides very finely hairy with prominent primary nerve, bluish-green. Flowers pentamerous, borne on bright reddish, curved pedicles up to 1" (1.5 cm) long. Sepals tiny and bright reddish; corollas rounded and jug-shaped, nearly ¼" (8 mm) long, light pink to whitish, and defined by small, recurved lobes around the opening. Capsules inconspicuous, brownish.
Blooming season:
May–June.
Occurrence: Prefers very wet, acid, peaty habitats, especially upland and transition bogs. Widespread in the bogs of northern and Central Europe, less common in the alpine boglands.
Identification tip: The plant has other common names: cankerroot, wild rosemary, rosemary-moorwort.
The oblong revolute leaves are characteristic.
Gardening tip: Not suitable for garden cultivation.

Alpine bearberry in fall

Red bearberry, flowers

During the brief period between fall and the onset of winter, the mats of Alpine bearberry produce incredible spectacles of color in the high mountain ranges. The richness of the color is influenced by the great differences between daytime and nighttime temperatures.

Red bearberry, fruits

Alpine Bearberry

Arctostaphylos alpina
Ericaceae
Appearance: Creeping deciduous dwarf and low-spreading shrub, forming extensive mats. Leaves oval, wedge-shaped at base, about 1" to 2" (2–5 cm) long, with reticulate venation on both sides. Flowers greenish-white or reddish. Berries red at first, aging to black, inedible.
Blooming season: May–June. Fruit ripening in September.
Occurrence: In Arctic and Alpine heathlands with dwarf shrub vegetation.
Identification tip: Look for venation visible on both sides.
Handsome fall colors.

Red Bearberry, Kinnikinick

Arctostaphylos uva-ursi
Ericaceae
Appearance: Very densely branched evergreen dwarf or low-spreading shrub with prostrate, mat-forming branches.
Leaves fairly large and very firm, sessile or short-stalked, oval, obtuse and rounded or slightly emarginate, upper surfaces glossy, undersides showing distinctly reticulate venation.
Flowers pentamerous, short-stalked, with jug-shaped, whitish, greenish, or pink-tinged corolla.
Berries inedible.
Blooming season: March–June.
Occurrence: Heathlands with dwarf shrub vegetation in the Arctic tundra and the Alps.
Identification tip: The reticulate venation on the undersides of the leaves distinguishes the plant from the similar-appearing mountain cranberry.
Gardening tip: Ground cover for alpine gardens. Needs a sunny site.

Ericaceae

Irish heath in flower

Irish heath, large bell-shaped flowers

This particularly handsome plant from the heathland regions of extreme Atlantic western Europe bears striking hanging corollas shaped like jugs. They are visited primarily by bumblebees.

Irish Heath, Connemara Heath, St. Dabeoc's Heath

Daboecia cantabrica
Ericaceae
Appearance: Evergreen dwarf shrub, with wide-spreading but open branches, erect or ascending, about 12" (30 cm) high.
The leaves are densely borne, alternate (sometimes also approximately opposite), and short-stalked. On the same plant they vary greatly in size, narrow-linear to lanceolate, upper surfaces dark green and rough, undersides covered with whitish hair. The leaf margins are revolute,

as in many dwarf shrubs of the Ericaceae. This creates a calm area on the underside, obviously serving as protection against transpiration. The flowers are tetramerous and are borne at the terminals of the branches, in loose racemes having few blossoms. The corollas are oblong, jug-shaped to bell-shaped, up to ½" (1.5 cm) long, and bright rose-purple, with the short lobes not markedly different in color. Capsules inconspicuous, brownish.
Blooming season: July–September.

Occurrence: In the wild, Irish heath occupies a very small range. It occurs only in heathlands near the coast, in northern Portugal, northern Spain, and Brittany to western Ireland. Cultivated in North America.
Identification tip: The inflorescences cannot be confused with those of any other species.
Gardening tip: Irish heath is available in several cultivars for heath gardens, but it is only conditionally hardy.

Ericaceae

Marsh rosemary, inflorescences

In previous times, the strongly aromatic marsh
rosemary was used in place of hops to give
flavor to beer—with a devastating effect,
because all the parts of this handsome plant are
slightly poisonous.

Marsh rosemary in its habitat

Marsh Rosemary
Ledum palustre
Ericaceae

Appearance: Usually very heavily branching evergreen wild shrub, tending to be verticillate, with erect stems and branches, about 3' to 5' (1–1.5 m), solitary or aggressive in fairly large stands. Young shoots covered with feltlike, rust-red hairs. Leaves stalked, leathery, lanceolate or linear, up to 1½" (4 cm) long and about ½" (1 cm) wide, upper surfaces dull olive-green, undersides rust-red, woolly to feltlike, leaf margins markedly involute.

The flowers are borne in profusion in erect terminal racemes drawn together like heads. The pentamerous corollas of the single flowers, spreading out in star shapes, are pure white, up to nearly ½" (1.5 cm) across, and shorter than the white stamens. Capsules inconspicuous, brownish. All parts of the plant exude a very strong aroma when crushed between one's fingers and are **mildly poisonous!**

Blooming season: May–June.

Occurrence: Prefers upland, transition, and woodland bogs from Newfoundland to Alaska.

Identification tip: Labrador tea *(Ledum groenlandicum),* available in garden centers, is very similar. Its leaves are roughly twice as long as wide and thus more oval in shape than those of our native marsh rosemary.

Gardening tip: Garden cultivation difficult and ecologically indefensible, because it would require peaty soil. Valuable source of nectar.

Blueberry in fall

Blueberry, flowers

Blueberry, fruits

Blueberry, Whortleberry, Bilberry, Whinberry
Vaccinium myrtillus
Ericaceae
Appearance: Usually profusely branching, densely leaved deciduous small shrub, up to 20" (50 cm). The stems become extremely woody only at the base. The branches are very firm, flexible, squared, and green. Leaves short-stalked, about ¾" to 1" (2–3 cm) long, oblong-oval, acuminate, rounded at base, margins finely dentate, dull light green. In fall, gorgeous golden-yellow to crimson.

Flowers with jug-shaped to bell-shaped corolla, greenish-white or bright red, borne singly or in pairs in the leaf axils, especially near the terminals of the branches. Berries very juicy, blue-black, with lighter frostlike bloom. Edible.
Blooming season: May–June. Fruit ripening in July.
Occurrence: From the lowlands to the mountains, especially in thin stands of conifers on acid, loose soils, in bog and heath regions, and in the dwarf shrub communities of the alpine region and the Arctic.

Identification tip: The squared, green branches and the light green leaves, which are neither leathery nor stiff, are characteristic.
Gardening tip: Blueberry shrubs are well suited to semishady spots in the garden. The fruits are relished by songbirds and small mammals as well. The closely related **swamp** or **high-bush blueberry** (*Vaccinium corymbosum*), up to 6½' (2 m) high and native to North America, is also sold for garden use.

115

Ericaceae

Bog whortleberry, flowers

Mountain cranberry, flowers

Bog whortleberry, fruits

Mountain cranberry, fruits

Bog Bilberry
Vaccinium uliginosum
Ericaceae
Appearance: Deciduous dwarf shrub, up to about 30" (75 cm). Leaves stalked, oblong-oval, rounded, up to 1" (2.5 cm) long, upper surfaces dull green, undersides blue-green.
Flowers have jug-shaped corolla, reddish at base. Berries up to ½" (1 cm) across, globular, with colorless juice, blue frostlike bloom. Edible.
Blooming season: May–July. Fruit ripening in August.
Occurrence: In upland bogs, marshy woods, coniferous stands, and heathland with dwarf shrub vegetation in the high mountains. Widespread in northern North America.
Identification tip: Unlike the blueberry, it has rounded, brown branches.
Gardening tip: Poorly suited to garden cultivation.

Mountain Cranberry, Cowberry
Vaccinium vitis-idaea
Ericaceae
Appearance: Evergreen dwarf shrub, up to 12" (30 cm). Leaves short-stalked, up to nearly 1" (2 cm) long, elliptic to oval. Flowers in hanging racemes, with jug-shaped, pink-tinged corolla. Berries globular, up to ½" (1 cm) across, initially whitish, aging to scarlet. Edible.
Blooming season: May–July. Fruit ripening in August.
Occurrence: Bog edges, open coniferous forests, and heathland with dwarf shrub vegetation in the high mountains.
Identification tip: The leaves of the similar bearberry have distinctly netted (reticulate) veins underneath.
Gardening tip: Mountain cranberries need an open site.

Ericaceae

Bogberry, single flowers

Bogberry, fruits

Bogberries are a small shrub. Their threadlike branches attract attention only when the disproportionately large berries are produced. The plant is rare in some areas.

Bogberry, Moorberry, Fen Berry, Small or European Cranberry

Oxycoccus palustris
Ericaceae

Appearance: Prostrate and creeping evergreen dwarf shrub with tiny, threadlike trunks and ascending, very thin stems, up to 32" (80 cm) long.

Leaves short-stalked, oblong-oval, acuminate, upper surfaces dark green and shiny, undersides covered with a blue-green frostlike bloom, only about ¼" × ½" (5 × 10 mm) in size.

The flowers are borne singly or in fours or fives in loose terminal racemes. They are tetramerous, pale pink or brighter reddish, and the corolla lobes, parted to the base, are recurved.

The fruits are yellow or beet-red juicy berries, large in relation to the size of the plant and reaching a diameter of ½" (1 cm). Edible.

Blooming season: May–July. Fruit ripening in August.

Occurrence: Only in upland bogs in the wettest spots, on cushions of peat moss. Widespread, but rare, from lowland areas to an altitude of 4280' (1300 m) in the mountains.

Identification tip: This plant cannot be mistaken for any other dwarf shrub. The globular and very inviting-looking fruits taste rather sour. They were gathered and eaten primarily in Scandinavia.

Gardening tip: Not suitable for garden cultivation.

Alder buckthorn, flowers

Alder buckthorn is considered an indicator of wetness. Its fruits are poisonous! Although the bark has great medicinal value, you should not attempt to use it on your own. The shrub is particularly valuable for wildlife.

Alder buckthorn, fruits in various states of ripeness (poisonous!)

Alder Buckthorn
Rhamnus frangula
Rhamnaceae

Appearance: Usually somewhat slender, thornless, medium-sized deciduous shrub or small tree with brown-red, wart-dotted bark on its branches and stems and gray-brown, longitudinally fissured outer bark on the trunk, about 6½' to 19½' (2–6 m).
Leaves smooth-margined, stalked, oval, broadest in their top third.
Flowers inconspicuous, greenish-white, borne singly or in small numbers in the leaf axils.

The globular drupes are green at first, passing through various yellow stages to red, aging to dull-lustered black.
Poisonous!
Blooming season: May–June. Fruit ripening in August.
Occurrence: Forest paths, margins of stands of woody species, thickets in bottom land and mixed coniferous stands, prefers acid water-logged soils.
Identification tip: Unlike the similar-looking common buckthorn of Europe (*Rhamnus cathartica*), the leaves of this plant are smooth-margined and the branches are always thornless. In addition, alder buckthorn leaves always have more than five pairs of lateral veins.
Gardening tip: Valuable wild shrub. The leaves feed, among others, the caterpillars of some butterflies and lycaenids; the nectar-rich flowers provide food for bees, flies, and beetles; the ripe drupes are consumed primarily by thrushes and other fruit-eating songbirds. Tolerates semishade.

Smoke tree in fruit

Smoke tree in flower

Smoke tree in fall

Smoke Tree, Smokebush, Burning Bush, Venetian Sumac

Cotinus coggygria
Anacardiaceae

Appearance: Profusely branching deciduous medium-sized shrub with outspread stems and branches, about 6½' to 16½' (2–5 m). Leaves long-stalked, broad-oval to rounded-elliptic, about 1" to nearly 3" (3–7 cm) long and up to 2½" (6 cm) wide, obtuse at the tips, rounded or slightly emarginate, thin, upper surfaces light or bright green, undersides bluish, both sides hairless.

The yellowish-white flowers are pentamerous, small, inconspicuous, and in large part sterile. They are profusely produced in loose terminal panicles up to 8" (20 cm) long. By the time they ripen in fall, the flowerstalks elongate and develop a dense covering of feathery hairs. They also turn reddish to purple-red.

Blooming season: May–July. Fruit ripening in October.

Occurrence: In the eastern Mediterranean region from the Balkan peninsula through the Near East to Central China, mostly in open, warmth-loving sunny thickets and woods on limy stone. Escaped in North America.

Identification tip: The distinctive fruit structures, which become considerably larger as they mature, are unmistakable.

Gardening tip: Frequently used as ornamental. Light-loving woody plant, (largely) hardy in Central Europe and temperate North America. Producing striking crimson foliage in autumn.

119

Polygalaceae/Chenopodiaceae

Milkwort in flower

Sea purslane at the edge of a tideway

Sea purslane in flower

Sea purslanes can tolerate saltwater. The stands are reminiscent of the far taller mangroves (tidal forests) on tropical coasts.

Milkwort, Polygala
Polygala chamaebuxus
Polygalaceae
Appearance: Prostrate, profusely branching evergreen subshrub, singly or in fairly small groups, up to 12" (0.3 m). Leaves leathery, short-stalked, elliptic to lanceolate.
Flowers borne singly or in twos in the leaf axils or at the terminals of the branches. Sepals winglike, creamy white or yellowish. Petals variable, yellowish or rose-red.
Blooming season: March–May.

Occurrence: Mountain-pine stands, dry mountain forests, stony meadows, or vegetation growing on rock debris, often in association with *Erica herbacea.*
Identification tip: The flowers resemble a wide-open papilionaceous flower.
Gardening tip: For sunny, dry rock and alpine gardens.

Sea Purslane
Halimione portulacoides
Chenopodiaceae
Appearance: Very bushy evergreen subshrub with ascending stems, up to 20" (0.5 m). Leaves on lower part of plant approximately opposite, at top of plant alternate, ovate, plump, gray-green, short-stalked. Flowers small, yellowish-green, in axillary and terminal racemes.
Blooming season: July–September.
Occurrence: Salty, muddy soils, coastal salt meadows, frequently along edges of tideways.
Identification tip: In the similar *Halimione pedunculata,* all the stalks are herbaceous.
Gardening tip: Not suitable for garden cultivation.

Ear willow shortly before flowering

Purple osier, male catkins

Ear willow during leaf production

Purple osier, release of air-borne seeds

Ear Willow
Salix aurita
Salicaceae
Appearance: Wide-spreading deciduous shrub, appearing fairly compact, with erect stems, up to 6½' (2 m) high.
Leaves with stalk ½" (1 cm) long, oval, widest in the upper half, with slender tip turned to the side or curved back, both sides hairy. Flowers dioecious, appearing before the leaves in catkins, ¼" to 1" (0.5–3 cm) long.
Blooming season: March–May.
Occurrence: Banks, edges of ditches, wet meadows, lowland bogs.
Identification tip: The large, ear-shaped stipules to which the plant owes part of its name (*aurita*) are especially characteristic.
Gardening tip: Suitable for wet soils along bodies of water in gardens.

Purple Osier
Salix purpurea
Salicaceae
Appearance: Very bushy large deciduous shrub, to about 20' (6 m), more rarely also small tree.
Leaves lanceolate, up to 10 times as long as wide, widest point above the middle. Flowers borne in unisexual catkins, about 2" (5 cm) long, appearing before the leaves.
Blooming season: March–April.
Occurrence: Along bodies of water, in stands of woody species in wooded meadows.
Identification tip: The hairless, slightly shiny branches are usually purple-red on the sunny side.
Gardening tip: Suitable for planting along the edges of relatively large bodies of water in gardens.

121

Salicaceae

Goat willow, male catkins

Gray sallow, male catkins

Goat willow, female catkins

Gray sallow, female catkins

Goat Willow, Sallow
Salix caprea
Salicaceae

Appearance: Usually loosely branching large deciduous shrub up to about 10' (3 m) or small tree. Leaves with stalks about ½" to 1" (1–2 cm) long, oval, rounded or faintly cordate at the base, undersides covered with dense, downy hairs. Flowers unisexual (dioecious) in catkins, appearing well before the foliage, up to about 1" (3 cm) long.
Blooming season: March–May. Fruit ripening in May.
Occurrence: Widespread in wild vegetation, along woods

edges on fallow land; also in open gravel pits and quarries.
Identification tip: The oval leaves are broadest in their lower halves.
Gardening tip: Prefers moist, loamy, nutrient-rich soils. Also thrives in semishade.

Gray Willow
Salix cinerea
Salicaceae

Appearance: Thick-stemmed, wide-spreading medium-sized deciduous shrub up to about 10' (3 m) high or small tree. Leaves short-stalked, oblong-oval, initially heavily covered with gray feltlike hairs, later

becoming hairless, upper surfaces gray-green, undersides bluish. Flowers borne in erect catkins, male up to 2" (5 cm) long, female up to 3½" (9 cm) long.
Blooming season: March–April.
Occurrence: Naturalized along ditches, in spring-fed swamps and alder swamps, common from the flatlands to the mountains.
Identification tip: The annual branches are covered densely with gray feltlike hairs. Hybridizes with other species.
Gardening tip: Prefers sandy-gravelly soils.

Salicaceae

Salix triandra, male catkins

The narrow-leaved willows that grow near bodies of water are usually hard to identify. In addition, they often hybridize with each other and produce myriad hybrid forms.

Hoary willow in its habitat

Almond Willow

Salix triandra
Salicaceae
Appearance: Densely branching large deciduous shrub, often appearing hemispherical in shape, up to about 13' (4 m), occasionally also small tree. Leaves stalked, oblong-elliptic, broadest in the center, margins very finely dentate, upper surfaces glossy dark green, undersides bluish-green. Flowers borne in unisexual catkins, 2" to 3" (6–8 cm) long, appearing with the leaves.
Blooming season: April–May.
Occurrence: Fairly common along stream and river banks (wooded meadows with shrub willows), from the flatlands into the high mountains. Cultivated in North America.
Identification tip: Male flowers with only three stamens (five or more in other species).
Gardening tip: Recommended for plantings at the edges of bodies of water in gardens.

Hoary Willow

Salix elaeagnos
Salicaceae
Appearance: Large deciduous shrub, about 10' to 20' (3–6 m). Leaves short-stalked, narrow-lanceolate or linear, initially covered with white feltlike hairs on both sides, later becoming hairless. Leaf margin revolute. Flowers unisexual (dioecious), in catkins.
Blooming season: April–May.
Occurrence: Mostly in small stands on gravelly soil.
Identification tip: The leaves are strikingly slender.
Gardening tip: Suitable for planting at the edges of bodies of water in gardens.

Salicaceae

Wideleaf dwarf willow in a stand

These small willow species are among the most impressive mat-forming low-spreading shrubs of the European high mountain ranges. Sometimes they are not even as tall as a match.

Netvein dwarf willow in a stand

Wideleaf Dwarf Willow
Salix herbacea
Salicaceae
Appearance: Low-spreading deciduous shrub with creeping, usually underground stem, 1" to 2" (2–5 cm). Leaves stalked, almost orbicular or oval, glossy medium green on both sides. Flowers appearing with or after the leaves. Male catkins globe-shaped, about ¼" (5 mm) in size; female catkins headlike, with few flowers, and up to about ½" (1 cm) long.
Blooming season:
June–August.
Occurrence: High mountains above the timber line up to about 9843' (3000 m), on seepage-damp, lime-free soils.
Identification tip: Reticulate venation obvious on the undersides of the leaves.

Netveined Dwarf Willow
Salix reticulata
Salicaceae
Appearance: Low-spreading deciduous shrub with prostrate stems that hug the ground and put forth roots, about 2" (5 cm) high. Leaves stalked, rounded, tips slightly emarginate, upper surfaces dark green and markedly wrinkled, undersides gray-green, with very prominent netted veins and long hairs. Flowers in dense, unisexual catkins, up to about 1" (3 cm) long, purple.
Blooming season:
July–August.
Occurrence: High mountains above the timber line up to 9217' (2800 m), also among mountain pines and Alpine rose. Alps, Pyrenees, Jura Mountains, and in Scotland.
Identification tip: The obviously indented netted veins on the wrinkled foliage leaves are very typical.
Gardening tip: Like the wideleaf dwarf willow, not suitable for garden cultivation.

Sand willow in fruit

Sand willow, male catkins

Creeping willow, flowering stand

Creeping willow, female catkin

Sand Willow
Salix arenaria
Salicaceae
Appearance: Deciduous shrub with bushy branches and creeping, mostly underground trunk, up to about 3' (1 m). Leaves short-stalked, elliptic, short-acuminate, with five to eight pairs of lateral veins, both sides covered with appressed hairs and having silky gleam. Catkins appear shortly before leaves, male catkins about ½" (1 cm) long, female up to about 1½" (3.5 cm).
Blooming season: April–May.

Occurrence: In lowland bogs, wet meadows, perennial-herb vegetation, and sand dunes outside hilly country.
Identification tip: The very similar *Salix repens* has leaves with four to six pairs of lateral veins.
Gardening tip: Suitable for windbreak plantings.

Creeping Willow
Salix repens
Salicaceae
Appearance: Dense, bushy small deciduous shrub with creeping trunk and prostrate or ascending stems, up to about 3' (1 m). Leaves short-

stalked, elliptic or lanceolate, with four to six lateral veins, gray-green. Flowers borne in catkins, appearing shortly before the leaves, male a little more than ½" (1.5 cm) long, female a little less.
Blooming season: April–May.
Occurrence: Lowland bogs, wet and unfertile meadows, coastal dunes. Widespread in Europe. Cultivated in North America.
Identification tip: Specimens occurring along the Baltic coast and bearing narrower leaves are sometimes recognized as a separate species, *Salix rosmarinifolia*.

125

Solanaceae

Boxthorn in flower

Boxthorn, flower and fruit (poisonous!)

The five stamens are clustered tightly at the center of the box-thorn flower to form a dispersion cone, which visiting insects find difficult to open.
All parts of the plant are poisonous.

Boxthorn, Duke of Argyll's Tea Tree
Lycium barbarum
Solanaceae
Appearance: Thorny, medium-sized deciduous shrub, about 3' to 10' (1–3 m). Branches erect, later also drooping, rod-shaped, longitudinally grooved, with lateral, often thorny short shoots. Leaves alternate and borne in profuse tufts along the leafy short shoots, narrow-elliptic, initially hairy, later becoming hairless, stalked, acuminate, both sides gray-green, highly variable in size and shape even on the same branch. Flowers borne singly or in small numbers in the leaf axils, long-stalked. Corolla light violet to red-violet (frequently yellowish after pollination), funnel-shaped, with narrow base and five-lobed outspread limb. Stamens white, much taller than the corolla. Berries elliptic, ½" to 1" (1–2 cm) long, shiny red when ripe, **poisonous!**
Blooming season: August–October. Fruit ripening in September.
Occurrence: Native to China, introduced to southern or Central Europe in the early eighteenth century and since escaped from cultivation, along walls, near ruins, or in places with rock debris. Likes growing near settled areas.
Identification tip: The flowers, produced in high-contrast colors on long, thin, twiggy branches, are unmistakable.
Gardening tip: When in flower and bearing fruit, boxthorn is very decorative and thus deserves to be used more widely.
The caterpillar of the death's-head moth feeds on its leaves. Prefers dry, sunny sites.

Butcher's broom in fruit

Butcher's broom, single flower

The spiny-pointed, leaflike leaf structures of this plant are in reality flattened branchlets. The true leaves are scalelike and small.

Butcher's Broom, Box Holly

Ruscus aculeatus
Liliaceae

Appearance: Dense, profusely branching small evergreen shrub with stiff, erect stems, about 3' (1 m). The dark green organs on the stems, which look like normal foliage leaves, are extremely flattened, broadened lateral branches (cladodes or cladophylls). They are arranged in two rows in a common plane and equipped with unpleasantly spiny tips. They are produced in the axil of the true leaves, which in this case are extremely tiny, simplified, and scalelike. The unisexual flowers, about ⅛" (2 mm) across, are dioecious. They are borne singly in the axils of the tiny scalelike leaves and apparently emerge from the center of the leaflike cladode. Berries greenish at first, later becoming bright coral red, about ½" (1–1.5 cm) in diameter. Inedible.

Blooming season: March–April.

Occurrence: In thickets and open to semi-shady woods of the Mediterranean region and the Canary Islands. In western France (Brittany) and parts of Great Britain, escaped from garden cultivation and naturalized. Cultivated in warm temperate United States.

Identification tip: The sharp-pointed cladodes, which assume the tasks of normal foliage leaves, are unmistakable. Dried specimens are popular in dried bouquets.

Gardening tip: Occasionally also grown for ornamental use.

Identifying Color: Green

Shrubs with Simple, Crenate, Lobed, or Sinuate Leaf Margins

Many shrubby woody plants are not content with the simple line of a smooth leaf margin, but instead display far greater diversity of margin design. They exhibit an astonishingly large number of different patterns, ranging from finely dentate and more coarsely serrate through irregularly crenate to deeply sinuate. A virtually inexhaustible multitude of possibilities is available in combination with the various forms of the basic leaf shape, from elongated and narrow with parallel margins all the way to almost perfectly spherical.

For these reasons, the list of species in this morphological group is especially extensive.

The dwarf birch is one of the characteristic species of the Nordic tundra. In Central Europe its gorgeous fall colors can be experienced only in relict communities.

French maple, ripe winged fruits

French maple

Amur maple, ripe winged fruits

Amur maple, fall foliage

French Maple
Acer monspessulanum
Aceraceae
Appearance: Loosely branching large deciduous shrub or small tree, about 10' to 20' (3–6 m), rarely to almost 33' (10 m), with slanting trunks and spreading, crooked main stems. Branches firm and not very flexible. The long-stalked leaves are divided into three lobes of roughly equal size, about 1" to 2½" (3–6 cm) long and up to about 3" (8 cm) wide, upper surfaces dark green with a dull luster, undersides lighter gray-green and covered with a sprinkling of hairs or only with axillary beards. In autumn the foliage takes on very bright orange or crimson tones. The flowers appear with or shortly after the leaves; they are yellowish-white and are borne in small numbers in umbellike racemes. The olive-brown or brighter reddish winged fruits, borne in pairs on the same pedicel, point upward and are almost parallel.
Blooming season: April–May. Fruit ripening in October.
Occurrence: Rocky slopes, open, sunny woods, preferably on limy soils. Common primarily in southern Europe and western Asia. The northern limit of its natural range runs through the northern Middle Rhine region. There it is also commonly known as castle maple, because it occurs in an area where many of the Rhineland's elevated strongholds are located.
Identification tip: The regular, three-lobed leaves are unmistakable.
Gardening tip: Decorative woody plant in parks and gardens, for sunny or semi-shady sites where winters are mild. Also tolerates being cut back.

Aceraceae

Hedge maple, fall foliage

The three maple species presented on these pages illustrate the great diversity of form of the leaf shapes in this genus of woody plants. While Amur maple produces oblong-oval leaves, French maple bears very regularly three-lobed leaves. In hedge maple, the leaf blades are more strongly articulated than in most of the other species.

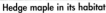

Hedge maple in its habitat

Amur Maple
Acer tataricum
Aceraceae
Appearance: Usually multi-trunked large deciduous shrub with profuse branching, about 13' to 20' (3–6 m), sometimes also small tree.
Leaves long-stalked, rounded-oval. Flowers greenish-white, appearing after the leaves. Winged fruits (samaras) ruby-red, nearly parallel.
Blooming season: May–June.
Occurrence: Rocky slopes, stands of woody species on banks, open deciduous forests from the lowlands to the mountainous regions. South-eastern Europe and Asia Minor. Frequently used as ornamental woody plant.
Identification tip: The leaves are not divided into lobes. Leafstalks covered with matted hair.
Gardening tip: Decorative broad-leaved shrub or tree for sunny locations.

Hedge Maple, Field Maple
Acer campestre
Aceraceae
Appearance: Heavily branching and usually leafy multi-trunked large deciduous shrub, about 13' to 20' (4–6 m), or taller tree. Leaves divided into three large and two smaller lobes, which are crenate and sinuate, upper surfaces dull dark green, undersides lighter and somewhat hairy. Bright yellow autumn color. Flowers yellow-green, appearing with the foliage in umbellike panicles. Winged fruits.
Blooming season: May.
Occurrence: Meadowland stands of woody plants, field hedges, thickets, woods edges. Widespread in Europe.
Identification tip: The long leafstalks contain milky sap.
Gardening tip: Outstanding shelter for birds.

131

Bigleaf hydrangea, cultivar

Bigleaf hydrangea, cultivar

In many hydrangea forms, only a few sterile flowers develop into large, showy organs. As a result, the whole inflorescence becomes a superflower.

Asiatic hydrangea

Bigleaf Hydrangea, French Hydrangea, Hortensia

Hydrangea macrophylla
Hydrangeaceae

Appearance: Densely bushy ornamental deciduous shrub with erect, thick branches, usually about 3' (1 m). The leaves are short-stalked and broad-lanceolate to oval, wedge-shaped or rounded at the base, tips slender-pointed, margins evenly dentate. Upper surfaces dull glossy green, undersides lighter and sparsely hairy. The lateral pinnae are arching. Flowers in hemispherical umbellike panicles. Corolla flattened, four-lobed, up to 2" (5 cm) across, in a wide color range from pure white to bluish and purple-red.

Blooming season: June–August.

Occurrence: Native to East Asia (Japan, China).

Identification tip: Homozygous specimens with the features of the wild plant are unlikely to be seen in park grounds and gardens. The forms raised in gardens or also as pot plants produce unusually luxuriant inflorescences, consisting predominantly of sterile flowers. In some cultivars the sterile flowers, developed for striking decoration of the corymb, form an outer wreath, while the other (inconspicuous) flowers are fertile.

Gardening tip: Grown in numerous cultivars as an ornamental woody plant. Bigleaf hydrangeas prefer sunny, open sites.

Hydrangeaceae

Climbing hydrangea, inflorescence

Bigleaf hydrangea, cultivar

Climbing hydrangea

Asiatic Hydrangea, Panicle Hydrangea

Hydrangea paniculata
Hydrangeaceae
Appearance: Deciduous ornamental shrub, about 3' to 13' (1–4 m).
Leaves long-stalked, occasionally also in threes at a common node, oblong-oval. Flowers copious in conical terminal panicles up to 12" (30 cm) long. Marginal (ray) flowers up to about 1½" (3.5 cm) across. Corollas yellowish-white or pure white, slightly reddish when faded.
Blooming season: August–September.

Occurrence: Native to East Asia.
Identification tip: Branches and undersides of leaves covered with stiff hairs.
Gardening tip: Several cultivars grown for ornamental use. Tolerates semishade.

Climbing Hydrangea

Hydrangea petiolaris
Hydrangeaceae
Appearance: Straggling, densely leaved deciduous climbing shrub. Climbs like ivy, with the help of aerial roots, on walls or tree trunks, up to about 33' (10 m).
Leaves broad-oval to rounded, 2" to 4" (5–10 cm) long, abruptly pointed, evenly serrate, upper surfaces shiny dark green and hairless. Flowers white, borne in profusion in large corymbs up to 10" (25 cm) across. Marginal flowers distinctly larger and up to about 1" (3 cm) across.
Blooming season: June–July.
Occurrence: Native to East Asia (Japan to Korea). Frequently cultivated for ornamental use.
Identification tip: On older branches the bark peels in layers.
Gardening tip: Also thrives in very shady places.

Hydrangeaceae

Sweet mock orange in flower

Sweet mock orange, single flowers

The large flowers of sweet mock orange, with their numerous stamens, are productive sources of pollen. They are visited primarily by bees and bumblebees, more rarely by pollen-gathering beetles.

Sweet Mock Orange, Garden Mock Orange
Philadelphus coronarius
Hydrangeaceae

Appearance: Medium-sized deciduous ornamental shrub with erect stems and rod-shaped branches with soft pith, about 3' to 10' (1–3 m). The opposite leaves are very short-stalked, oval, acuminate, rounded at the base, irregularly dentate, upper surfaces dark green and hairless, undersides lighter and with hairy veins. The tetramerous flowers are stalked, borne in upright axillary racemes primarily at the terminals of the branches. Petals pure white, about 1" to 1½" (3–4 cm) across, spread out flat or in bowl shapes, exuding a very intense fragrance (especially toward evening).
Brownish capsular fruits.

Blooming season: May–June.

Occurrence: Woods edges, sunny, open thickets, sunny mountain slopes. From the southeastern Alps and Tuscany to western Asia. Naturalized in North America.
Very popular ornamental woody plant, frequently cultivated, but growing wild in only a few places.

Identification tip: Hybrids produced by crossing with East Asian or North American species also are found on the market; they resemble the European sweet mock orange in many features and are not easy to differentiate.

Gardening tip: The heavily scented flowers are reminiscent of jasmine. **True jasmine** (*Jasminum officinale*) has pinnate leaves composed of three leaflets and is not frost-hardy.

Forsythia, flowers

Twinflower

Forsythia, fall foliage

Twinflower, which usually grows no higher than the length of a finger, was given its scientific name in honor of the great Swedish botanist Carl von Linné, or Carolus Linnaeus.

Forsythia, Border Forsythia, Golden Bells
Forsythia intermedia
Oleaceae
Appearance: Deciduous shrub with hollow stems and lamellate pith, about 6½' to 16½' (2–5 m).
Leaves oblong-oval to lance-olate, long, smooth-margined or finely serrate. Flowers tetramerous, bright yellow.
Blooming season: April.
Occurrence: Native to East Asia; produced by crossing **weeping forsythia** *(Forsythia suspensa)* and **green-stemmed forsythia** *(Forsythia viridissima).*

Identification tip: The wild forms of the forsythias pro-duce two different types of flowers: either macrostylous (two-part stigma taller than the pollen sacs) or short-styled (pollen sacs taller than the stigma).
Gardening tip: Largely without value for wildlife.

Twinflower, Linnaea
Linnaea borealis
Caprifoliaceae
Appearance: Very delicate, almost herbaceous-looking dwarf shrub with thread-like but woody stems, to 6" (15 cm).

Leaves short-stalked, leathery and coarse, rounded. Flowers in pairs on long stalks, bell-shaped to funnel-shaped.
Blooming season: June–August.
Occurrence: Fairly rare in moss-rich coniferous forests and heathland with dwarf shrub vegetation on acid, vir-gin humus soils. In the high mountains of Europe as far as the Urals, also in Scandinavia.
Identification tip: Leafstalks are long-ciliate.
Gardening tip: Difficult for garden cultivation.

135

Caprifoliaceae

European cranberry bush, flowers

Leatherleaf viburnum, flowers

European cranberry bush, fruits (poisonous!)

Viburnum species are among the most attractive garden shrubs. Although the fruits look enticing, they are poisonous to humans. Only birds and small mammals can snack on them unharmed.

European Cranberry Bush, Guelder Rose, Snowball
Viburnum opulus
Caprifoliaceae
Appearance: Bushy deciduous wild shrub with outspread, somewhat drooping stems, about 3' to 13' (1–4 m). Leaves long-stalked, three- to five-lobed, upper surfaces dark green and hairless, undersides sparsely hairy. Flowers white, numerous, in terminal corymbs; ray (marginal) flowers with large, star-shaped corolla, sterile, central flowers smaller with bell-shaped corolla, fertile. Drupes bright red. **Mildly poisonous!**
Blooming season: May–June. Fruit ripening in August.
Occurrence: Borders of thickets, stands of woody species in meadows, frequently cultivated.
Identification tip: Leafstalks with conspicuous green nectar glands.
Gardening tip: Good shelter for birds. Sunny to semishady site.

Leatherleaf Viburnum
Viburnum rhytidophyllum
Caprifoliaceae
Appearance: Evergreen ornamental shrub with upright stems and branches, about 3' to 13' (1–4 m). Leaves oblong-oval, to 8" (20 cm) long, irregularly dentate, upper surfaces glossy dark green. Flowers white or yellowish. Inflorescences carried through winter.
Drupes red at first, finally turning black. **Poisonous!**
Blooming season: May–June.
Occurrence: Native to East Asia.
Identification tip: The heavily wrinkled leaves, covered on the underside with dense, felt-like hair, are unmistakable.
Gardening tip: Tolerates shade.

Wayfaring tree in a stand

Wayfaring tree, ripening fruits (poisonous!)

Weigela, single flowers

Wayfaring Tree
Viburnum lantana
Caprifoliaceae
Appearance: Bushy deciduous wild shrub with erect stems, about 3' to 13' (1–4 m). Leaves short-stalked, plump, but soft, sharp-toothed, dull green, undersides covered with gray, feltlike hair. Flowers white, in domed corymbs, without enlarged ray flowers. Drupes bright red at first, finally turning shiny black.
Poisonous!
Blooming season:
April–June. Fruit ripening in September.
Occurrence: Forest borders, open deciduous forests, thickets.
Identification tip: The finely wrinkled leaves are very soft to the touch.
Gardening tip: Frequently planted along streets. Very decorative and valuable shelter for birds.

Weigela
Weigela florida
Caprifoliaceae
Appearance: Moderately branching deciduous ornamental shrub, about 3' to 6½' (1–2 m).
Leaves oblong, acuminate, serrate, upper surfaces hairless, undersides hairy on veins. Flowers borne singly or in compact panicles in the leaf axils, pentamerous, funnel-shaped, up to 2" (5 cm) long, whitish, pink, or fairly bright reddish.
Blooming season: May–June.
Occurrence: Native to East Asia. In Central Europe, frequently grown for ornamental use.
Identification tip: The shoots and young branches have two hairy stripes.
Gardening tip: Very decorative, but of modest value for domestic wildlife.

Japanese barberry, flowers

Single shrub

Fall foliage

Fruit crop

Japanese Barberry
Berberis thunbergii
Berberidaceae
Appearance: Densely branched, bushy deciduous ornamental shrub, about 3' to 5' (1–1.5 m). Branches squared and covered with brown-red bark.

Leaves stalked, borne in tufts in the axils of long leaf thorns, oval to spatulate, up to about 1" (3 cm) long, remotely dentate, in the original form vivid green with bluish undersides, in the most commonly used garden variety tinged with purple-red, in autumn assuming brilliant scarlet. Flowers yellow, hemispherical, stalked, in hanging racemes. Sepals often reddish outside, up to ½" (1 cm) across. Berries oblong-oval, up to ½" (1 cm) in diameter, scarlet, inedible.

Blooming season: May–June.
Occurrence: Native to East Asia (Japan).
Identification tip: The evergreen, shiny leaves of **wintergreen barberry** *(Berberis julianae)*, which comes from China and is used as a shrub for parks and gardens, are far more strongly dentate. Numerous other deciduous or evergreen species of this genus are represented among the ornamental woody plants.
Gardening tip: Long in garden culture and very frequently used as a hedge plant in front yards. Japanese barberry suffers little damage from industrial and automotive exhaust gases. It is decidedly hardy and tolerates pruning, and consequently is often sheared to form monotonous box-shaped hedges (bearing few flowers). As a solitary shrub, valuable for domestic wildlife.

Berberidaceae

Common barberry, fruit

Common barberry flowers

Common barberry in fall

Barberries are especially valuable for many animal species. Their use in gardens is to be encouraged.

Common Barberry
Berberis vulgaris
Berberidaceae
Appearance: Erect, thorny deciduous wild shrub with arching stems, about 3' to 10' (1–3 m). Shoots squared and longitudinally striped, conspicuously light green-gray. Leaves stalked, arranged in tufts and hence often apparently opposite, oblong-elliptic, long wedge-shaped at base, tips rounded or acuminate, margins with sharp, thorny teeth, upper surfaces dark green, undersides lighter, hairless, up to 1½" (4 cm) long, with strong midrib. Flowers with yellow sepals and petals, hemispherically domed, in hanging racemes. Berries oblong, up to ½" (1 cm), bright red, edible, very sour.
Blooming season: April–June. Fruit ripening in September.
Occurrence: In thickets, meadowland hedges, forest borders, in clearings, and on dry slopes; thrives in limy, unfertile soils. Except in northern Europe, very common, from the lowlands up to about 6592' (2000 m).
Identification tip: The leaves of the long shoots are modified into multiparted spines (leaf thorns) up to nearly 1" (2 cm) long, in whose axils short shoots arise. The six yellow stamens abruptly bend toward the center of the flower when you touch their base with a pointed blade of grass.
Gardening tip: Barberry, as an intermediate host of black wheat rust, has been eradicated in many areas.
Valuable and also very decorative sheltering plant for birds. Loves sunny locations.

139

Alpine currant, inflorescences

Golden currant flowers

Alpine currant fruit

Many species of the *Ribes genus* bear rather inconspicuous flowers such as those of Alpine currant, which also appears in lowland regions. Golden currant flowers are strikingly colorful, however.

Alpine or Mountain Currant
Ribes alpinum
Grossulariaceae
Appearance: Unarmed, densely branched, bushy deciduous wild shrub, about 3' to 6½' (1–2 m).
Leaves stalked, rounded in outline, three- to five-lobed, somewhat shiny, hairless. Flowers greenish-yellow, in erect racemes, frequently dioecious, female inflorescences having few flowers. Berries scarlet, edible, bland-tasting.
Blooming season: April–June. Fruit ripening in August.

Occurrence: Thickets, open woods, forest borders, lowland wooded meadows, and stony hillsides in mountainous areas.
Identification tip: Leafstalks fringed with long glandular hairs.
Gardening tip: Tolerates semishade and exhaust gases.

Golden Currant
Ribes aureum
Grossulariaceae
Appearance: Deciduous ornamental shrub, about 3' to 10' (1–3 m). Leaves deeply trilobed, hairless, wine-red in autumn. Flowers golden-

yellow, borne in erect or spreading racemes, fragrant. Berries pea-sized, black, edible.
Blooming season: April–May. Fruit ripening in June.
Occurrence: Native to California. Frequently cultivated and in some places growing wild.
Identification tip: Easily identifiable by the golden-yellow flowers and the hairless, dull-lustered three-lobed leaves.
Gardening tip: Popular ornamental shrub for sunny to semishady sites.

Grossulariaceae

European black currant, flower

Rock currant

European black currant, fruit

Currant flowers are rich in nectar, and for this reason they are popular with bees, bumblebees, and other hymenopterous insects. For humans, gathering the fruits is not worth the effort, because the taste is inferior to that of the cultivars.

European Black Currant

Ribes nigrum
Grossulariaceae
Appearance: Deciduous shrub, about 3' to 6½' (1–2 m). Leaves long-stalked, upper surfaces hairless, undersides with yellow glands. Flowers greenish-yellow, in spreading or hanging racemes. Sepals longer than petals. Berries globular, black, juicy, edible.
Blooming season: April–May. Fruit ripening in June.
Occurrence: In meadows and in damp thickets on banks of bodies of water. Widespread in Europe.

Identification tip: When crushed, leaves and bark smell strongly aromatic.
Gardening tip: In garden culture since the sixteenth century; many high-yielding cultivars in use. Tolerates semishade. Berries also provide food for birds.

Rock Currant

Ribes petraeum
Grossulariaceae
Appearance: Usually rather heavily branching deciduous wild shrub, about 3' to 6½' (1–2 m). Leaves long-stalked. Flowers borne in groups in spreading or hanging racemes, reddish. Berries globular, red, very sour-tasting, edible.
Blooming season: April–May. Fruit ripening in June.
Occurrence: In mountain forests and stream ravines. Cultivated in United States.
Identification tip: Leaves covered with dense white hair beneath.
Gardening tip: Little used in garden culture, recommended for natural gardens (rock gardens).

Red currant, cultivar

Red currant, standard variety

Common gooseberry

Red Currant

Ribes rubrum
Grossulariaceae
Appearance: Deciduous berry bush with erect stems, about 3' to 6½' (1–2 m). Leaves long-stalked, multi-lobed, flowers greenish-yellow or reddish, in hanging racemes.
Berries globular, pea-sized, scarlet, edible.
Blooming season:
April–May. Fruit ripening in June.
Occurrence: Originally a plant of wooded meadows and thickets on banks.
Identification tip: Flower-ing or winter currant *(Ribes sanguineum)*, which has large, light-red racemes, is an ornamental shrub native to North America.
Gardening tip: Popular berry bush. For sunny and semishady sites.

Common Gooseberry

Ribes uva-crispa
Grossulariaceae
Appearance: Bushy decidu-ous wild shrub with erect, prickly branches, 20" to about 5' (0.5–1.5 m).
Leaves three- to five-lobed, deeply crenate or dentate, in tufts, hairy. Flowers greenish or green-purple, borne singly or in racemes with few flowers.
Berries rounded, up to 1" (2 cm), greenish, bristly-haired, with translucent longi-tudinal striping, edible.
Blooming season: April–May. Fruit ripening in July.
Occurrence: As wild plants in wooded meadows and open thickets. Widespread in Europe.
Identification tip: The branches are bristly.
Gardening tip: Very popular berry bush. No special soil requirements.

Hedgerow thorn, single flower

Hedgerow thorn

Hedgerow thorn in fruit

Hedgerow Thorn, Singleseed Hawthorn

Crataegus monogyna
Rosaceae

Appearance: Densely branching, thorny deciduous wild shrub, about 10' to 16½' (3–5 m), or small tree. Leaves long-stalked, deeply trilobate or multilobed, upper surfaces dark green, both sides hairless. Flowers white, borne profusely in corymbs, unpleasantly scented, containing only one ovary (style). Pomes with a single stone, red, somewhat sour, inedible.
Blooming season: May–June. Fruit ripening in September.

Occurrence: Widespread in hedges, thickets, along forest borders and on slopes. Frequently in cultivation.
Identification tip: In *Crataegus laevigata*, the upper portions of the leaves are trilobed (more rarely, five-lobed) or merely deeply crenate; the sinuses do not extend as far as the center of the leaf. Flowers with two ovaries (styles). Blooms earlier than the sister species, but otherwise resembles it in many features.
Gardening tip: Both *Crataegus* species make excellent woody plants for hedges,

because they tolerate pruning well. With their abundant flowers and fruits, their effect is highly decorative. Important as food and habitat for numerous small animals native to this country (insects, songbirds, small mammals) and thus highly recommended as a shelter plant not only for the open countryside, but for relatively large gardens and parks as well.

143

Showy crab apple, single flowers

Showy crab apple, fruits

Showy crab apple, a free-flowering woody plant for gardens

Cultivar 'Golden Horst'

Showy Crab Apple, Flowering Crab

Malus floribunda
Rosaceae

Appearance: Many-stemmed, wide-spreading deciduous ornamental shrub with erect and spreading stems, about 6½' to 10' (2–3 m), sometimes distinctly taller.

The long-stalked leaves can reach a length of about 1" (3 cm). They are broad- or oblong-elliptic, with clearly pointed tips, broad wedge-shaped or rounded at the base, with awned teeth and indistinctly lobed. The lateral veins extend as far as the larger teeth of the leaf margins. Only the undersides of the leaves are hairy.

Flowers pentamerous, very numerous, in simple umbels at the terminals of short shoots; deep red in bud, opening to deep pink outside and almost pure white within. Pomes very small, about ½" (1 cm) thick, indented at the base of the fruitstalk, orange-red to deep red-cheeked. Taste is tart and somewhat sour; inedible raw.

Blooming season: April–May. Fruit ripening in September.

Occurrence: The wild form of this apple is unknown; it was introduced from Japan in the form of a cultivated plant and/or ornamental plant.

Identification tip: In addition to showy crab apple, which is very popular because of its abundance of flowers, numerous other hybrids and cultivars are planted as ornamental shrubs or trees. It is very difficult to assign them more precisely.

Gardening tip: Undemanding in terms of soil requirements. The flowers are valuable as food for lepidoptera and bees. The fruits are eaten by thrushes.

Wild apple

Wild apple, crab apples

Most cultivars have taken on a characteristic of wild apple. The outsides of the petals are brighter pink and reddish. In extremely rare cases they are pure white, as in other native wild fruit species.

Wild Apple, Common Crab Apple
Malus sylvestris
Rosaceae
Appearance: Somewhat thorny, wide-spreading deciduous wild shrub or small tree, about 16½' to 33' (5–10 m). Leaves long-stalked, rounded to broad-lanceolate in shape, serrate, short-acuminate, upper surfaces finely wrinkled, both sides initially covered with dense, short hairs, upper surfaces later turning to a dull, glossy dark green, undersides finally becoming almost hairless. Yellow-brown in fall. Flowers borne in clusters on long stalks along short shoots, pentamerous. Corolla up to 1½" (4 cm) across, spreading out flat, inside white, outside reddish. Pomes the size of ping-pong balls, greenish-yellow, tasting bitter and somewhat sour.
Blooming season: May. Fruit ripening in September.
Occurrence: In thickets, meadowland hedges, woody plants in fields, and along bodies of running water. Prefers nutrient-rich, fresh loamy and stony soils. Widespread in Europe where sometimes also planted in open fields for grazing game.

Identification tip: The rounded-oval leaves and the widespreading branches are typical. Nonetheless, not easy to distinguish from naturalized cultivars.
Gardening tip: Not highly recommended for garden cultivation. The ecological value of high-trunked cultivated varieties of *Malus* for domestic wildlife, especially in an open meadow of dehiscent fruit-bearing trees, is greater. The flowers, leaves, and fruits are a rich source of nourishment. Holes in the trunks and main stems are desirable places in which to live or rest.

145

White dryas

White Dryas, Mountain Avens
Dryas octopetala
Rosaceae

Appearance: Evergreen dwarf shrub growing only 4" (10 cm) high, with prostrate, mostly creeping stems and branches. Forms mats or carpets over relatively large areas (low-spreading shrub). Leaves long-stalked, up to about 1" (3 cm) long and ½" (1 cm) wide, elliptic, cordate at base, tips acute, heavily crenate, leathery, upper surfaces wrinkled, bright green, undersides densely covered with silvery hairs. Leaf margin usually somewhat involuted. Flowers borne singly, long-stalked, conspicuous and large, up to about 1½" (4 cm) across, with usually eight broad-oval, pure white or creamy white petals. The styles lengthen when fruiting occurs, becoming feathery-haired tails that aid in wind dissemination.

Blooming season: May–August. Fruit ripening in July.

Occurrence: Dwarf shrub vegetation of the Arctic tundras and moraine debris, rocky fields and meadows above the timberline in the high mountain ranges of Europe.

Identification tip: The stipules are fused with the leaf-stalk over more than 50 percent of their length. The eight-sided corolla cannot be confused with any other species.

Gardening tip: The very free-flowering, decorative white dryas is sold for use in rock gardens. It tolerates no shade or competition from other plants. As far as the soil requirements are concerned, it is largely undemanding, however.

Valuable nectar plant for insects.

146

Japanese kerria, double-flowered form

Double flowers are far more eye-catching and decorative, of course, but ecologically they are unsuitable, because their nectar and pollen usually are sterile.

Japanese kerria

Japanese Kerria
Kerria japonica
Rosaceae

Appearance: Profusely branched deciduous ornamental shrub with long, erect, twiggy stems, 20" to 6½' (0.5–2 m). The branches have vivid green bark and are filled with whitish pith tissue. Leaves stalked, oblong-oval, broad wedge-shaped or cordate at base, tips long-pointed, upper surfaces hairless and bright green, undersides slightly hairy.

Flowers borne singly or in small numbers in the leaf axils at the terminals of leafy shoots, up to about 1" (3 cm) across, brilliant golden-yellow, with five rounded, flat-spread petals. The garden varieties produce mostly double flowers compressed into headlike shapes; they are sterile, but in other features resemble the wild variety.

Blooming season: May–June, in some years again in September–October.

Occurrence: Native to East Asia (China), where it occurs as undergrowth in open deciduous forests. Naturalized in North America.

Identification tip: The slightly shiny, light green branches and the oblong, doubly serrate leaves are unmistakable.

Gardening tip: Popular for many years, and commonly planted as an ornamental shrub. Japanese kerria has become naturalized and proved very resistant to exhaust fumes and thus is often planted in industrial regions or urban front yards. When free-standing, numerous suckers quickly develop. Also tolerates shade.

Rosaceae

Purple-leaved plum, cultivar 'Nigra'

Purple-leaved plum, fruits

Purple-leaved plum, ripe drupe

Purple-leaved Plum, Cherry Plum, Myrobalan Plum

Prunus cerasifera
Rosaceae

Appearance: Very wide deciduous shrub or multi-trunked small tree, about 13' to 26' (4–8 m). Young branches glossy green, reddish on the sunny side, hairless, later covered with gray-brown bark and sprinkled with tiny pores. Sometimes also thorny. Leaves long-stalked, oblong-oval to elliptic, up to nearly 3" (7 cm) long, acuminate, wedge-shaped at base, crenate or irregularly serrate, upper surfaces glossy dark green, hairless, undersides lighter. The long-stalked flowers appear shortly before or during leaf production. They are pure white, about 1" (2 cm) across, and are borne singly (rarely also in numbers) along short shoots. Drupes about 1" (2–3 cm) in size, globular, green at first, later turning yellow, reddish, or brown-red. Edible and very pleasant-tasting.

Blooming season: March–April. Fruit ripening in August.

Occurrence: Widespread from the Balkans to the Near East. Long in cultivation as a fruit tree.

Identification tip: Resembles sloe somewhat, but can be differentiated by its larger flowers and statelier growth.

Gardening tip: Prefers sites with full sun or little shade, on limy loess.

Frequently used as an ornamental, especially in a red-leaved variety. Supposedly original form of Syrian plum.

Rosaceae

Dwarf Russian almond

Dwarf Russian almond, ripening fruits

European dwarf cherry, ripening drupe

Dwarf Russian Almond

Prunus tenella
Rosaceae
Appearance: Dense, leafy deciduous shrub with twiggy, erect stems, 20" to about 3' (0.5–1 m), produces runners. Leaves oblong-oval, acuminate, sharply serrate. Flowers borne singly in the leaf axils, rose-red. Drupes cherry-sized, covered with gray felt-like hairs, inedible. **Seeds poisonous!**
Blooming season: March–May. Fruit ripening in August.
Occurrence: In thin woods, thickets, and vineyard borders from southeastern Europe (Lower Austria) to Siberia.
Identification tip: Leaves almost sessile, stiffly upright.
Gardening tip: Decorative ornamental woody plant for sunny, dry sites. Productive honey-yielding plant.

European Dwarf or Ground Cherry

Prunus fruticosa
Rosaceae
Appearance: Thornless, wide-spreading deciduous shrub, 20" to about 3' (0.5–1 m). Leaves stalked, oval to elliptic, with obtuse tips, serrate or crenate. Flowers long-stalked, borne profusely in compact umbels, pure white.
Drupes globe-shaped, beet-red to black-red. Edible.
Blooming season: April–May. Fruit ripening in June.
Occurrence: Thickets, dry slope locations, path borders, open quarries, sunken roads.
Identification tip: The small, glossy leaves are characteristic.
Gardening tip: Highly suitable as an ornamental plant for stony soils in sunny positions.

149

Mahaleb cherry, flowers

Ripening drupes

Mahaleb cherry, ripe drupes

The glossy black drupes of mahaleb cherry, also known as St. Lucie cherry, are edible, but picking them generally is not worth the effort. It is better to leave them for birds.

Mahaleb or St. Lucie Cherry
Prunus mahaleb
Rosaceae
Appearance: Wide-spreading deciduous wild shrub or small, but always multi-trunked tree, about 3' to 10' (1–3 m), with very broad, outstretched, branchy top. Young branches covered with fine, downy hair, somewhat gummy, gray, with very light pores.
Leaves long-stalked, rounded-oval, 1" to 1½" (2–4 cm) long and almost as wide, rounded or slightly cordate at the base, with green-ish nectar gland, tips short-pointed, upper surfaces glossy dark green, undersides dull, lighter green. Flowers produced with the leaves, in multiples in stalked erect or spreading racemes. Petals pure white, oblong, tips rounded, very fragrant. Drupes pea-sized, globular, not very juicy, reddish at first, aging to black with dull lus-ter. Edible.
Blooming season: April–May. Fruit ripening in August.
Occurrence: In thin thickets on rocks and in woods, on dry, very sunny and stony slopes, or in lawn borders.

Common from the Iberian Peninsula to the eastern Mediterranean region.
Identification tip: The glossy, mostly hairless, and fairly small leaves, as well as the racemose inflorescences and fruit structures are unmistakable.
Gardening tip: Valuable as a shelter for birds.
Not suitable for semishady sites!

Sloe as flowering hedge in meadowland

Sloe, ripe drupes

Sloe, flowering branch

Sloes are decidedly early bloomers. Long before other meadowland woody plants, they produce flowers and change the appearance of the fields. After the first frost in fall, the ripe fruits are popular—not only with the larger songbirds.

Sloe, Sloe Tree, Blackthorn

Prunus spinosa
Rosaceae

Appearance: Very dense-stemmed and wide-spreading deciduous wild shrub with spreading or erect stems and branches covered with short stem thorns, about 3' to 10' (1–3 m), rarely also higher. Leaves borne in tufts, stalked, elliptic to oval, acuminate or obtuse, serrate and crenate, dull dark green.

The pentamerous flowers appear quite some time before the leaves; they are borne in profusion along the short shoots all over the shrub, about ½" (1–1.5 cm) wide, pure white. The ovary is located at the base of a cup-shaped structure. Drupes globe-shaped, initially bluish-green, aging to blue-black with a lighter frostlike bloom. Edible, but very high in tannin before the first relatively severe frosts. Often retained on the boughs during the winter.

Blooming season: March–April. Fruit ripening in October.

Occurrence: Very common in the borders of woods and thickets, in stands of woody plants in fields, and in meadowland hedges, along the edge of vineyards, and in relatively dry riverside meadows. From the flatlands to the low mountains, around 4921' (1500 m).

Identification tip: The short shoot thorns, up to 2" (5 cm) long and protruding at right angles, the slightly wrinkled leaves, and the clustered fruits are unmistakable features.

Gardening tip: Ideal shelter plant for birds, for sunny, dry edges.

151

Firethorn, cultivar

Firethorn

Occasionally some cultivars of the handsome firethorn bush bloom a second time in early fall. Then the same shrub bears ripening fruits and newly opened flowers simultaneously, although these flowers do not mature thoroughly. The inviting fruits are edible, but the seeds they contain are not!

Firethorn, Everlasting Thorn
Pyracantha coccinea
Rosaceae
Appearance: Wide-spreading semi-evergreen shrub with spreading and erect stems and thorny short shoots, about 3' to 10' (1–3 m). Leaves short-stalked, oblong-lanceolate to oblong-oval, on long shoots 2" to 3" (5–8 cm) long, on short shoots 1" to 1½" (2–4 cm) long and up to ½" (1.5 cm) wide, leathery, coarse, tips obtuse or short-spined, dentate, upper surfaces glossy dark green, undersides lighter, dull, and hairy only on the larger veins, retained on the shrub through the winter without changing color, shed in following spring and replaced by new leaves. Flowers copious, borne in stalked, mostly erect, flattened corymbs about 1" to 1½" (3–4 cm) across. Corolla pentamerous, creamy white to reddish-yellow.
Pomes (spurious fruits) roughly pea-sized, globular, red-orange or beet-red.
Thought to be poisonous.
Blooming season: May–June, occasionally a second time in September–October. Fruit ripening in September.

Occurrence: Native to south-eastern Europe from Italy through the Balkans to the Black Sea region, where firethorn is found in woods edges or meadowland hedges.
Identification tip: The long shoot thorns and the characteristic fruit structures are unmistakable.
Gardening tip: Since the seventeenth century, also in cultivation in Central Europe owing to its decorative flowers and fruit. Tolerates shearing into hedge shape. Valuable shelter for birds. Especially for sunny sites on loamy or stony soils.

Wild pear in flower

Wild pear, ripe fruits

Wild pear in its habitat

Wild Pear

Pyrus pyraster
Rosaceae

Appearance: Wide-spreading and slightly thorny deciduous wild shrub, about 6½' to 13' (2–4 m), or as a tree, up to about 66' (20 m).

Leaves long-stalked, leafstalk sometimes as long as the leaf blade, which is rounded-oval to broad-elliptic, serrate on the upper two-thirds of the margin, broad wedge-shaped to rounded at the base, tips short-pointed, upper surfaces slightly glossy and dark green, undersides bluish-green, both sides covered with fine hairs only at the outset. Flowers pentamerous, long-stalked, several in umbels at the terminals of leafy short shoots, calyx with feltlike hair, petals pure white, sometimes slightly tinged with pink. In contrast to the apple blossom, the five styles are parted all the way to the base. Pomes stalked, rounded to oblong-oval, yellow-green to brown-yellow. Edible, but very tart.

Blooming season: April–May. Fruit ripening in September.

Occurrence: Sporadic and never in a stand, in thickets, hedges, and open mixed forests on sunny slopes, also in riverside vegetation of woody plants. From the flatlands to the higher mountains. Very common in Europe.

Identification tip: Thorny shoots, relatively small leaves, and woody fruits distinguish the wild pear from escaped cultivars.

Gardening tip: As wild fruit tree, significant for a number of fruit-eating animals. Undemanding.

Mountain ash, ripe fruits

Like the fruits of the arborescent *Sorbus* species, those of mountain ash are valuable primarily to birds. Frequently they are harvested by winter visitors only after the first heavy frosts.

Mountain ash, shortly before flowers open

Mountain Ash, Dwarf Whitebeam

Sorbus chamaemespilus
Rosaceae

Appearance: Bushy, loose-branched deciduous wild shrub, about 3' to 6½' (1–2 m). Singly or in small stands. Leaves stalked, elliptic to oblong-ovate, tips obtuse or spiny-pointed, serrate, upper surfaces hairless and glossy, leaf veins covered with tiny dots, undersides bluish-green and covered with thin hairs. Flowers drawn together in dense, white-felted corymbs with rose-red petals. Pomes oblong, deep orange-red or brown-red. Edible, but very mealy.

Blooming season: June–July. Fruit ripening in August.

Occurrence: Mostly in coniferous forests (stands of pines and larches), in mountain-pine belts, Alpine rose thickets, and vegetation of *Alnus viridis* in the high mountains of Europe, also in the Black Forest and the Vosges.

Identification tip: The similar *Sorbus mougeotii* also grows in the form of a shrub. Its leaves have dark green upper surfaces, densely white-felted undersides, regularly lobed or sinuate margins. The flowers are white. Occurs in the mountain forests of southwestern Europe as well as through the entire Alpine chain to the Carpathians. Both species produce hybrids at a common site, and will cross-pollinate with other species of the same genus.

Gardening tip: The shrubby mountain ashes are not commonly available commercially for garden use. For sunny sites.

Spiraea chamaedrifolia, stand

Douglas spirea, inflorescence

Douglas spirea belongs to the same morphological group as bridewort. The shrubs and trees used in parks and gardens include a great many other species and forms—for example, *Spiraea chamaedrifolia*, with its profusion of white flowers.

Bridewort, stand

Bridewort, Spirea
Spiraea salicifolia
Rosaceae
Appearance: Bushy, heavily branching deciduous ornamental shrub with very slender erect or arching, usually dense-leaved stems, about 3' to 6½' (1–2 m).
Leaves stalked, oblong-lanceolate, tips obtuse or short-acute, with very small stipules at the base, unevenly serrate, hairless, upper surfaces somewhat darker. Flowers borne in profusion in erect, soft-haired terminal panicles up to 4" (10 cm) long and triangular in shape.

Sepals with margins curled back, corolla pentamerous, reddish-white.
Blooming season: June–July.
Occurrence: Native to East Asia.
Identification tip: Easily recognizable by the willow-like leaves and the free-flowering panicles.
Gardening tip: Bridewort has long been cultivated as an ornamental woody plant with great diversity of form, no special requirements in terms of site or soil, tolerates trickling moisture and temporary flooding. Because of especially vigorous root growth,

contributes to rapid fixation of slope soils or escarpments. Of minor significance for native wildlife, except as a source of nectar and pollen for bees and other insects. Also suitable for semishady sites.

155

Rosaceae

Japanese spirea in garden use

Japanese spirea

Spireas are popular as ornamentals, principally for their free-flowering panicles and long blooming season. You will rarely see pollinating insects on their luxuriant flowers.

Japanese Spirea
Spiraea japonica
Rosaceae
Appearance: Very bushy deciduous ornamental shrub with erect stems and branches, about 20" to 5' (0.5–1 m).
Leaves elliptic, slender-pointed, wedge-shaped at base, up to 4" (10 cm) long, doubly serrate, upper surfaces dull green, undersides bluish, hairless. Flowers in flat corymbs at the terminals of the branches, bright pink or purple.
Blooming season: June–August.

Occurrence: Native to East Asia (Japan).
Identification tip: Numerous other species in a virtually unsurveyable and hard-to-differentiate field of cultivars are in garden use. Among the white-flowering species, *Spiraea chamaedrifolia* looks very similar. Another very common species is Douglas spirea *(Spiraea douglasii)*. Its flowers are borne in erect slender panicles, and its leaves have white-felted undersides.
Gardening tip: In cultivation as an ornamental woody plant for many years. Garden cen-

ters usually offer not the homozygous species, but hybrids. Very productive summer bloomer. Tolerates semishade and is remarkably frost-hardy. Suitable for solitary plantings as well as background use and bordering of garden beds. Very undemanding in terms of soil requirements.
Of little significance for wildlife, except for flower-visiting insects like flies, syrphid flies, and wild bees.

English ivy, flowers

English ivy, old (almost treelike) specimen

Ivy, fruits (poisonous!)

English Ivy
Hedera helix
Araliaceae
Appearance: Evergreen climbing shrub, creeping on the ground or covering walls and trees by means of aerial rootlets, up to about 66' (20 m). Often with clearly discernible main trunk, otherwise very bushy-branched and densely leaved. Leaves of two types. Along non-flowering shoots, three- to five-lobed, cordate at the base, glossy dark green with a whitish network of veins; along flowering shoots, diamond-shaped to elliptic, unlobed or perhaps slightly undulate. In winter, the undersides of the leaves are tinged with red, while the upper surfaces are black-green. Flowers bisexual, inconspicuous, small, but very numerous, borne in long-stalked umbels forming headlike mounds.
Berries globular, distinctly flattened at the tip, dull black. **Poisonous!**
Blooming season: September–October. Fruit ripening the following spring.
Occurrence: Common in woods and thickets, riverside vegetation, quarries, and ruins. From the flatlands to the low mountains.
Identification tip: Unmistakable.
Gardening tip: Climbing shrub to cover walls and sides of houses. Very shade-tolerant.
The unusually late blooming date ensures insects an abundant supply of nectar in fall. The fruits are relished by songbirds. Important as nesting site and hiding place.

157

Malvaceae/Hamamelidaceae

Rose of Sharon

Red-flowered cultivar

Blue-flowered cultivar

Rose of Sharon, Shrub Althea

Hibiscus syriacus
Malvaceae
Appearance: Moderately branching deciduous ornamental shrub, about 3' to 6.5' (1–2 m).
Leaves stalked, three-lobed. Flowers borne singly in the leaf axils, funnel-shaped to bell-shaped, up to 2½" (6 cm) across, in the wild form pure white with reddish base, in garden forms usually pink, purple, light blue, or blue-violet.
Blooming season: July–September.

Occurrence: Native to East Asia (originally the Near East was assumed to be the place of origin, hence the scientific name *syriacus*).
Identification tip: The corolla is twisted in a spiral inside the flower bud.
Gardening tip: Long in widespread use, in many cultivars. By and large undemanding.

Spike Winter Hazel

Corylopsis spicata
Hamamelidaceae
Appearance: Deciduous ornamental shrub with erect or drooping stems, 20" to 6½' (0.5–2 m).

Leaves ovate, pointed at tips, both sides dull green and largely hairless.
Flowers appearing before the leaves, light yellow, in hanging spikes up to 1½" (4 cm) long.
Blooming season: March–April.
Occurrence: Native to East Asia.
Identification tip: The leaves are like hazel leaves, but much smaller.
Gardening tip: Used as an early bloomer in parks and gardens. Not shade-tolerant, otherwise undemanding.

Aquifoliaceae

Spike winter hazel in flower

English holly, male flowers

Spike winter hazel, single flowers

English holly, fruits

English Holly, Common Holly

Ilex aquifolium
Aquifoliaceae

Appearance: Usually very dense-leaved evergreen shrub with erect stems and branches, about 3' to 16½' (1–5 m), more rarely also small tree. Sometimes forming stands. Branches and twigs green.

Leaves stalked, very firm, leathery, and coarse, oblong-oval, five or more long, thorny spines on each edge with margins shallow or deeply sinuate between, tips acute, rounded at base, upper surfaces glossy dark green, undersides dull light green, hairless. Flowers unisexual (dioecious), inconspicuous, with white corolla sometimes also with reddish tinge. Drupes approximately pea-sized, globular, scarlet, many-seeded. **Poisonous!**

Blooming season: May–June. Fruit ripening in October.

Occurrence: In undergrowth of open deciduous forests and thickets in Atlantic Europe.

Identification tip: The spiny-tipped evergreen leaves are characteristic.

Gardening tip: The tree form usually develops only when the plant is free-standing. Numerous cultivars with differently colored foliage are commercially available. As a wild plant, offers shelter and cover. The flowers provide nectar for hymenopterous insects. The fruits are relished by thrushes.

159

Myricaceae

Sweet gale in its habitat

Male catkins

Sweet gale with catkin buds

As early as late summer, the slender red-brown catkins appear in the leaf axils. They do not bloom until the following spring. Stands of sweet gale look very lovely during the blooming season.

Sweet Gale, Bog Myrtle
Myrica gale
Myricaceae
Appearance: Profusely branching, bushy deciduous wild shrub with erect, twiggy stems and branches, 20" to about 3' (0.5–1 m). Usually in stands. Branches densely dotted with resin glands, exuding a very strong, pleasantly aromatic scent when stripped off or rubbed between one's fingers. Leaves short-stalked, firm and somewhat leathery to the touch, oblong-oval, thorny-toothed near tip, acuminate, wedge-shaped at base, upper surfaces dull green, undersides grass-green, both sides thinly covered with appressed hairs. Flowers unisexual (dioecious), borne in erect, compact, axillary catkins, opening long before leaves. Drupes brownish and inconspicuous. **Poisonous!**
Blooming season: March–May.
Occurrence: On wet, boggy sandy and peaty soils in heath moors and damp heaths, in the border of lowland and highland bogs, and along ditches. Atlantic western and northern Europe from Portugal to Norway.

Identification tip: The characteristic scent and the toothed leaves make confusion with *Ledum palustre* impossible. In earlier times the branches were used to flavor beer.
Gardening tip: Not suitable for garden cultivation. The leaf and flower buds provide food for black grouse during the winter.

Fagaceae

Evergreen beech, leaves

Downy oak in its habitat

Evergreen beech in its habitat

Downy oak in fruit

Evergreen Beech, Southern Beech

Nothofagus antarctica
Fagaceae
Appearance: Deciduous shrub or many-trunked small tree, 10' to 20' (3–6 m). Leaves very short-stalked, in two dense rows, oval, upper surfaces glossy dark green, undersides lighter and hairless. Flowers inconspicuous, greenish.
Blooming season: May.
Occurrence: Native to southern Chile (Tierra del Fuego).
Identification tip: The two-rowed foliage produces a fishbone pattern.

Gardening tip: Frequently used as an ornamental woody plant in parks and relatively large gardens.
Tolerates semishade, can be clipped to create hedge.

Downy Oak

Quercus pubescens
Fagaceae
Appearance: Loosely branching deciduous wild shrub up to 16½' (5 m), more rarely also straight-trunked tree. Leaves stalked, ovate in outline, both edges having seven to nine rounded sinuses and lobes, wedge-shaped at base, later covered with soft

down only on the undersides. Flowers inconspicuous, yellowish-green.
Acorns up to about 1" (3.5 cm) long, broad-ovate.
Blooming season: April–May.
Occurrence: Very common in western and southern Europe.
Identification tip: The leaves resemble those of Durmast oak *(Quercus petraea)*, but their covering of soft hairs is a distinguishing feature.
Gardening tip: Prefers open, warm, temporarily dry sites.

Green alder, fruit structure

Green alder, small female and large male catkins

Green alder, stand

Green Alder
Alnus viridis
Betulaceae

Appearance: Many-stemmed deciduous shrub with wide-spreading stems and branches, 20" to about 8' (0.5–2.5 m). Usually in stands. Rarely also small tree. Leaves long-stalked, oval, acuminate, broad wedge-shaped or rounded at base, doubly serrate, 2" to 3" (5–8 cm) long, becoming gummy after leaf production, undersides glossy green, with brownish axillary beards. Flowers appearing with leaves, in unisexual inflorescences (monoecious), male catkins whitish-haired, hanging; female, about ½" (1 cm) long, upright at the terminals of the branches, reddish. Fruit structures cone-shaped.

Blooming season: April–May.

Occurrence: At subalpine altitudes in the area of the timberline, forms large pure stands on avalanche paths, in irrigated fields, and along stream courses. Also along woods edges and in wooded meadow vegetation at lower altitudes. In the European high mountain ranges up to 7875' (2400 m). In some mountainous regions, occa-sionally cultivated also to reinforce avalanche-threatened slopes.

Identification tip: The leaves, which have dull green surfaces with clearly acuminate tips, distinguish this species from the other two native and predominantly arborescent growing species, **common** or **black alder** (*Alnus glutinosa,* a lowland species) and **European gray alder** (*Alnus incana,* a species found in hilly country).

Gardening tip: Unsuitable for garden cultivation.

Betulaceae

Dwarf birch in fall foliage

Dwarf birch

Shrub birch in its habitat

Female catkin

Dwarf Birch

Betula nana
Betulaceae
Appearance: Highly
branched deciduous dwarf
shrub with prostrate or
ascending stems, about 20"
(0.5 m) high. Leaves very
short-stalked, almost round.
In fall turning golden-yellow
to reddish. Flowers in globular to oblong catkins.
Blooming season: April–May.
Occurrence: Prefers water-
logged peaty soils of upland
and lowland bogs. Forms
groves in the Arctic tundra. In
Central Europe, sporadic in
the northern lowlands, in low

mountain bogs, and in the
Alpine foothills.
Identification tip: The circu-
lar leaves are unmistakable.
Gardening tip: Use to edge
bodies of water in gardens.

Shrub Birch

Betula humilis
Betulaceae
Appearance: Profusely
branching deciduous wild
shrub, 20" to 6½' (0.5–2 m)
high. Leaves broad-oval or
rounded, always longer than
wide.
Flowers in erect catkins,
opening with the leaves.
Blooming season: April–May.

Occurrence: Prefers bog
meadows, thickets at bog
edges, and swampy woods of
willow and alder. In Central
Europe, only in a few places
in the Alpine foothills and in
the northern lowlands.
Identification tip: The
rounded leaves distinguish it
from younger specimens of
**European white or weeping
birch** *(Betula pendula)*
and **white birch** *(Betula
pubescens)*.
Gardening tip: Not suitable
for garden cultivation.

163

Betulaceae

European hazel, male flower

European hazel, unripe hazelnut

Red filbert, fruit

Corylus maximus, fruit

European Hazel, Common or European Filbert

Corylus avellana
Betulaceae

Appearance: Large, usually quite broad-growing shrub, singly or in fairly small groups, 6½' to 13' (2–4 m). Leaves short-stalked, doubly serrate, in outline rounded to obovate, with slender tip. Flowers appear long before the leaves: male flowers very numerous in light-yellow catkins, female flowers concealed in somewhat thickened buds, with long, deep red stigmas 1 or 2 millimeters long. Hazelnuts in a close-fitting husk, edible.

Blooming season: January–April. Fruit ripening in September.

Occurrence: At moderately dry places in borders of forests, in thickets, fields, and along bodies of running water.

Identification tip: *Corylus maxima,* native to southeastern Europe and Asia Minor, produces leaves up to 6" (15 cm) long and almost as wide. Its nuts are enclosed in a tubular husk, closed like a paper bag and narrowed at the top. This plant provides the hazelnuts (filberts) we see in stores. In parks we see the red-leaved variety commonly known as the **red filbert.** Another ornamental is the **American hazelnut** *(Corylus americana),* with the husk open, but longer than the nut.

Gardening tip: This hazel is well suited for larger gardens or mixed hedges (sun to semishade).

Valuable as a nesting site and food source for birds and small mammals.

Grapevine (Riesling)

Grapevine (Pinot Noir)

Grapevine, Grape, Wine Grape

Vitis vinifera

Vitaceae

Appearance: Deciduous shrub, climbs by means of tendrils, 33' to 66' (10–20 m) high. Leaves long-stalked, in outline rounded to cordate, three- to five-lobed, sharply dentate, upper surfaces hairless, undersides densely covered with hair. In fall (depending on cultivar), golden-yellow or deep red. Flowers inconspicuous, greenish-yellow, slightly scented, borne in profusion in erect or spreading panicles.

Sepals and petals fall very early; in the wild form, unisexual (dioecious), in cultivated vines predominantly bisexual. Berries globe-shaped, depending on cultivar yellow-green, red-brown, or blue-violet, edible.

Blooming season: June. Fruit ripening in September.

Occurrence: The wild form of grapevine is a liana found in wooded meadows, especially in the Mediterranean region.

Identification tip: The climbing shrub commonly known as **wild grapevine** (*Vitis sylvestris*) is one of the

most important original species of the cultivated vines. In cultivation since early antiquity, it now is available in numerous cultivars. In comparison to the wild grapevine, the cultivars produce thicker twigs, hairier leaves, and larger, juicier berries.

Gardening tip: Grapevines are excellent for covering house walls in sunny, dry positions. Largely undemanding in terms of soil requirements.

Identifying Color: Blue

Shrubs with Compound (Pinnate) Leaves

Shrubs with deeply divided and compound leaves go one step further in their leaf design than leaves with special leaf-margin features. They break down the leaf blade itself—which originally was a single piece or at most was divided into lobes by deep sinuses—into several portions, each of which looks like a separate leaf.

The individual sections of a compound leaf are called leaflets or pinnae. The same design features of the leaf margins found in the simple leaves appear once again in the leaflets, which occur in even or odd numbers. In addition to largely smooth-margined leaflets, there are others with dentate, serrate, crenate, or sinuate patterns.

Wild roses such as the dune rose do not confine their display of beauty to the blooming season. The finely cut foliage with the graduated leaflets is the very epitome of loveliness.

Alpine clematis, single flowers

Alpine clematis in its habitat

Usually the large bluish petals of Alpine clematis open only slightly, forming a large, bell-shaped single flower. The flower provides copious amounts of pollen for insects to eat.

Alpine Clematis
Clematis alpina
Ranunculaceae

Appearance: Deciduous left-hand twining shrub with long, flexible trunks and stems, rope-shaped in the manner of lianas, usually climbing only about 6½' to 10' (2–3 m) high. Leaves long-stalked, pinnate to bipinnate with three unpaired leaflets. Leaflets very short-stalked or sessile, lanceolate, pointed at tip, wedge-shaped at base, coarsely toothed, undersides slightly hairy. They support the long leafstalks by twining as the plant is anchored to the growing surface. Flowers, unlike those of *Clematis vitalba,* very large, long-stalked, pendulous, borne singly on short shoots in the leaf axils of the terminals of the branches. Floral envelope composed of four petals, out-spread in a star shape or drawn together in a bell shape, light blue or violet (rarely also white), and enclosing a circle of about 10 white nectar leaves (modified stamens). Style covered with feathery hair in ripe state.

Blooming season: May–July. Fruit ripening in September.

Occurrence: In semishady, vegetation-rich mountain forests, in Alpine rose and mountain pine thickets, and on overgrown slopes covered with rock debris and stands of tall herbaceous plants.

Identification tip: Unlike *Clematis vitalba,* flowers produce not only pollen, but also nectar.

Gardening tip: Not suitable for garden cultivation.

Traveler's joy, unripe fruits

Single flowers

Ripe fruit structure

Longitudinally fissured bark

Traveler's Joy, Common Clematis

Clematis vitalba
Ranunculaceae

Appearance: Densely branching deciduous twining shrub (liana) with long, flexible, left-hand twining stems, climbing to heights of over 33' (10 m). Trunks up to nearly 1" (2 cm) thick. The gray-brown bark peels off in long strips. Young twigs six-sided and longitudinally striped.

Leaves opposite, long-stalked, up to 10" (25 cm) long, imparipinnate. Five to seven leaflets, placed far apart, up to 2" (5 cm) long, smooth-margined or serrate, hairless, upper surfaces dull dark green, undersides somewhat lighter.

Flowers long-stalked, with four narrow, creamy white, hairy sepals, combined in loose axillary panicles. When ripe, the style becomes a silver-haired flying organ aiding in wind dissemination of the light nuts.

Blooming season: June–September. Fruit ripening in October.

Occurrence: Common in veil communities along stream and river banks, along woodland borders, in field thickets and hedges. Widespread in western and Central Europe. From the flatlands to over 4926' (1500 m).

Identification tip: Within the Ranunculaceae, one of the few genuses with opposite leaflets. The silver-white fruit structures look very decorative in late fall and winter, especially against the light.

Gardening tip: Highly recommended for large, near-natural gardens. Offers many small birds excellent opportunities for nesting and concealment. Shade-tolerant.

Jackman's clematis, blue variety

Anemone clematis, climbing on the side of a house

Jackman's clematis, red variety

Anemone Clematis, Mountain Clematis

Clematis montana
Ranunculaceae

Appearance: Deciduous twining shrub that climbs by means of its leafstalks and reaches heights up to about 50' (15 m). Branches rounded. Leaves long-stalked, trifoliolate. Leaflets with incised lobes and coarsely serrate, upper surfaces dull green. Flowers very handsome, up to 3" (8 cm) across. Like all *Clematis* species, lacks petals; floral envelope instead has pink-whitish or light reddish, petal-like sepals and tufts of yellow stamens.

Blooming season: May–June.

Occurrence: Native to the Himalayas.

Identification tip: In **Jackman's clematis** *(Clematis jackmanii)*, now available in many cultivars, the flowers grow even larger. This plant was developed through systematic crossing of the East Asian *Clematis lanuginosa* with the red-violet flowering *Clematis viticella,* native to southern Europe and western Asia. The flowers reach a diameter of almost 5" (12 cm) and often contain more than four violet-blue sepals.

Gardening tip: Very popular, frequently used, and quite early-blooming ornamental climbing plant. All clematis cultivars are superb for covering fences and walls, but they require a certain amount of care. They bloom luxuriantly, especially in sunny sites. The large-flowered garden cultivars, too, are valuable donors of pollen and nectar and are frequently visited by bees and lepidoptera.

Caprifoliaceae

European elder in its habitat, in flower

European elder, ripe fruits

Elder is a feast for the eyes, a special ornament, at almost every season of the year. As the fruits ripen, their stalks turn reddish, making the plant even more inviting to potential harvesters.

European Elder
Sambucus nigra
Caprifoliaceae
Appearance: Very bushy deciduous wild shrub with erect or overarching stems and branches, about 10' to 23' (3–7 m) high. More rarely also small tree with crooked trunk. Branches with white pith, covered at first with green bark, later turning light brown with numerous warty pores.
Leaves long-stalked, imparipinnate, with five to seven leaflets, which are almost sessile, elliptic, long-pointed, serrate, upper surfaces dull green, undersides hairless and lighter green. Unusually aromatic when rubbed between one's fingers. Flowers small, creamy white, very numerous, in large, flattened corymbs, with strong, very pleasant scent. Drupes (elderberries) globular, black-red with purple-red juice. **Poisonous when green**, edible when black.
Blooming season: May–June. Fruit ripening in August.
Occurrence: Very common shrub along woods edges, in stands of woody species in fields, along banks and fences. Nitrogen-loving plant. Widespread in Europe.
Identification tip: The soft white pith of the branches is very characteristic, even in the leafless state. The fruit-stalks turn beet-red in the ripe state.
Gardening tip: Valuable wild fruit tree, very decorative in all seasons. Flowers important as food for insects. The fruits are also very popular with numerous songbirds.

171

Red-berried elder, inflorescences

Red-berried elder in its habitat

Red-berried elder, fruits

Red-berried Elder, European Red Elder

Sambucus racemosa
Caprifoliaceae
Appearance: Moderately branching deciduous wild shrub with erect or slightly overhanging stems and branches, about 3' to 13' (1–4 m).

Leaves long-stalked, imparipinnate, 4" to 10" (10–25 cm) long, with usually five leaflets, which are narrow-lanceolate, overall much narrower than those of *S. nigra,* upper surfaces dull dark green, undersides bluish and with scant hair, exuding a strong, slightly unpleasant smell when rubbed between one's fingers. Often reddish-purple during leaf flush. Flowers small, light yellow, appearing with the leaves, pleasantly scented, very numerous in compact, erect oval panicles.

Drupes globe-shaped, roughly pea-sized, scarlet, juicy. Fruit edible only after being heated. Stones and other plant parts **slightly poisonous!**
Blooming season: April–May. Fruit ripening in July.
Occurrence: Widespread in Central and southern Europe, in open thickets, open coniferous forests and woods, vegetation in timber areas, meadowland shrubs and trees, and along paths and lanes. Mostly at lower and higher altitudes of low mountain ranges.
Identification tip: The pith of the branches is rust-red.
Gardening tip: Important shelter plant for birds. Recommended for garden hedges or as solitary specimen shrub. Can easily be grown from the stones.

Loves sunny to semishady sites on nutrient-rich loose soils.

Staphyleaceae

European bladder nut, flowers

European bladder nut, capsular fruits

Opened capsule

European Bladder Nut
Staphylea pinnata
Staphyleaceae
Appearance: Deciduous wild shrub with upright stems and limited branching, about 6½' to 16½' (2–5 m). Branches greenish at first, later becoming brown-reddish with numerous light lenticels. Leaves long-stalked, imparipinnate, up to 10" (25 cm) long, with usually five or seven leaflets, which with the exception of the terminal pinna are very short-stalked or sessile, elliptic and pointed, undersides bluish, both sides hairless, finely ser-

rate. Flowers pentamerous, sepals yellowish-white with slight reddish tinge, in shape and color indistinguishable from the petals, which are only slightly larger. The flowers are borne in hanging, loosely branching terminal panicles.
Capsular fruits globular or pear-shaped, inflated and papery, pale green, slightly wrinkled, up to 1½" (4 cm) long. Inedible.
Blooming season:
May–June. Fruit ripening in September.
Occurrence: In vegetation-rich mixed forests, along bor-

ders and in timber areas, likes lime-rich slopes. From the Swiss Jura through the northern edge of the Alps to the Carpathians and the Balkans.
Identification tip: The ripe seeds cause a rattling noise in the unusual inflated fruits.
Gardening tip: Interesting broad-leaved woody plant for stony sites that are warm in summer.

Berberidaceae

Holly mahonia, fruits (poisonous!)

The evergreen leaves of mahonia exhibit characteristic changes in color throughout the year. In winter they are usually brownish-red. A fungal infestation can cause them to turn beet-red, however.

Holly mahonia, flowers

Holly Mahonia, Oregon Holly Grape

Mahonia aquifolium
Berberidaceae

Appearance: Thornless. Moderately branching, dense-leaved evergreen ornamental shrub, 20" to 5' (0.5–1.5 m). Leaves long-stalked, impari-pinnate, with five to nine oblong-oval to elliptic leaflets, which are 1½" to 3" (4–8 cm) long, sessile except for the terminal pinna, with up to 10 lateral veins that end in sharp, thorny marginal teeth, sinuate between, very leathery and coarse, upper surfaces glossy dark green.

During the winter months, upper surfaces purple or beet-red. Flowers up to ½" (1 cm) across, with hemispheric floral envelope of golden-yellow sepals and petals, borne in profusion in hanging racemes up to 4" (10 cm) long, pleasantly scented.

Berries initially bluish green, ripening to blue-black and heavily covered with bluish frostlike bloom, juice dark red. **Mildly poisonous.**

Blooming season: April–May. Fruit ripening in September.

Occurrence: Native to northwestern North America. In places, growing wild and naturalized.

Identification tip: The hemispheric flowers each contain six sensitive stamens. If you touch them at the base of the filament of the anther with a sharp blade of grass or a needle, they instantly fold inward. That makes it easier for flower-visiting insects to take on a load of pollen.

Gardening tip: Very common ornamental woody plant in parks and gardens. A valuable source of food for insects as well as songbirds. Undemanding, also in semishade.

Field rose, flower

Field rose, fruits

Bush cinquefoil in flower

Bush Cinquefoil, Shrubby Cinquefoil
Potentilla fruticosa
Rosaceae
Appearance: Profusely branching deciduous ornamental shrub, up to about 3' (1 m).
Leaves stalked, palmately pinnate, with three to five leaflets. Leaflets about ½" (1 cm) long, sessile, oblong-lanceolate, acute at tip, wedge-shaped at base. Flowers pentamerous, borne singly at the terminals, with golden-yellow petals.
Blooming season: June–September.

Occurrence: In open woods, and rocky slopes from south-western to southeastern Europe. Frequently cultivated and in places naturalized.
Identification tip: The flowers contain large numbers of stamens.
Gardening tip: Easy to propagate by cuttings and undemanding soil requirements.

Field Rose
Rosa arvensis
Rosaceae
Appearance: Climbing deciduous wild shrub with drooping shoots, 20" to 6½' (0.5–2 m).

Leaves imparipinnate, with five to seven elliptic leaflets. Flowers solitary, long-stalked, pure white. Sepals fall early. Rose hips globular-oval, up to nearly 1" (2 cm) long, light red. Edible.
Blooming season: June–August. Fruit ripening in September.
Occurrence: Forest borders and thickets in the limestone regions of western and Central Europe.
Identification tip: The styles of the ovaries are fused into a column.
Gardening tip: For hedges on limy soil.

Dog rose in its habitat, in flower

Thorns on a branch

Uncommon red flowers

Ripe rose hips

Dog Rose

Rosa canina
Rosaceae

Appearance: Deciduous wild shrub, rounded when free-standing, otherwise climbing, with somewhat ramified stems, about 3' to 10' (1–3 m). Prickles of the branches uniform, mostly strongly hooked. Leaves stalked, imparipinnate, with five to seven leaflets. Leaflets very short-stalked, elliptic, up to 1½" (4 cm) long and nearly 1" (2 cm) wide, upper surfaces bright or dark green, dull, undersides slightly bluish, hairless or with fine silky hair, singly or doubly sharply serrate. Flowers borne singly or in threes on short stalks in the upper leaf axils, up to about 2" (6 cm) across, pale pink or reddish, rarely pure white, slightly fragrant.
Rose hips up to about 1" (2.5 cm) long, coral-red, hairless, edible.

Blooming season: June–July. Fruit ripening in September.

Occurrence: Roadsides, thickets, woody species in fields, hedgerows, woods edges, and unfertile pastures. In Central Europe, the most common wild rose by far, and found everywhere except in the far north.

Identification tip: The numerous styles are not fused to form a column in the center of the flower. The species is exceptionally rich in variety; it now is organized into about 60 small species, which are difficult to differentiate.

Gardening tip: This species, like the other wild roses, is recommended for near-natural gardens (primarily as a hedge shrub). From the bloom until the fruits ripen, it provides small wildlife with a great deal of food and a place to live.

May rose

French rose in flower

May rose rose hips

French Rose
Rosa gallica
Rosaceae
Appearance: Deciduous
(tending to be also semi-
evergreen) wild shrub with
arching branches, 20" to
about 3' (0.5–1 m).
Leaves imparipinnate, with
three to five leaflets, which
are coarse, rounded-elliptic.
Flowers mostly borne singly,
light red to dark purple.
Rose hips globular, brown-
red, edible.
Blooming season: June–July.
Fruit ripening in September.
Occurrence: Thickets and
open woods, borders of

unfertile and dry grassplots.
Central and southern Europe.
Identification tip: The pin-
nate sepals do not fall.
Gardening tip: See **dog rose**.

May Rose
Rosa majalis
Rosaceae
Appearance: Deciduous wild
shrub with runners and long,
twiggy stems, about 3' to 5'
(1–1.5 m).
Leaves with five to seven
leaflets, their upper surfaces
bluish green and covered
with appressed hairs, undersides gray-green and densely
hairy. Flowers solitary, pink-

white to crimson, up to about
2" (6 cm) across.
Rose hips globular, dark red,
edible.
Blooming season: May–June.
Fruit ripening in August.
Occurrence: Wooded meadows of the Alpine rivers, also
in southern Scandinavia and
in the northern Balkans.
Identification tip: The
sepals are very narrow and
undivided.
Gardening tip: For stony
soils in natural gardens.

Rosaceae

Slender spines

Dune rose rose hips

Dune rose in flower

Dune or pimpinella-leaved rose attracts attention by virtue of its especially large single flowers and black-reddish rose hips.

Dune Rose, Pimpinella-leaved Rose

Rosa pimpinellifolia
Rosaceae

Appearance: Very small deciduous wild shrub with runners, about 20" (0.5 m) high. Leaves stalked, with five to 11 leaflets. Flowers solitary, long-stalked, creamy white, yellowish at the center. Rose hips globular, black, edible.

Blooming season: May–June. Fruit ripening in August.

Occurrence: Scattered but aggressive in the dune regions of the North Sea and in thickets on rocks in the low mountains where summers are warm and naturalized in parts of North America.

Identification tip: Easily distinguishable from other wild roses by its very dense thorns and black rose hips.

Gardening tip: For bed edging or small hedges on dry soils.

Sweetbriar, Eglantine

Rosa rubiginosa
Rosaceae

Appearance: Deciduous wild shrub, about 3' to 10' (1–3 m). Leaves with five to seven leaflets, broad-oval to round, undersides dotted with dark glands.

Flowers borne singly or in small numbers in the leaf axils, light pink or vivid pink. Rose hips globe-shaped, deep orange-red, edible.

Blooming season: May–June. Fruit ripening in August.

Occurrence: Open thickets in sunny positions, fell fields. Widespread in Central and southern Europe.

Identification tip: The foliage leaves exude a very pleasant applelike or winey scent when stripped off.

Gardening tip: See **dog rose**.

Japanese rose in a stand

Sweetbriar flowers

Japanese rose, single flower with visitors

Japanese Rose
Rosa rugosa
Rosaceae
Appearance: Many-stemmed, very leafy deciduous ornamental and wild shrub with erect stems, about 3' to 5' (1–1.5 m).

Leaves stalked, imparipinnate, five to nine leaflets that are elliptic to oval, coarsely serrate, leathery and firm, upper surfaces crinkly, vivid or dark green, with indented veins, undersides lighter or gray-green and hairy. Stipules broad and serrate, with spreading auricles. Flowers solitary or in small numbers in loose umbellike racemes, deep rose or purple-pink, sometimes also pure white, up to 3" (8 cm) wide. Sepals hairless, erect, always undivided and smooth-margined. Rose hips very large, globe-shaped, wider than tall, very fleshy and soft, scarlet, edible.

Blooming season: May–August. Fruit ripening in August.

Occurrence: Native to East Asia. In many cases, growing wild and naturalized in coastal dunes or coastal heaths.

Identification tip: The stems and branches are very thickly covered with straight, thin prickles.

Gardening tip: Introduced to Central Europe around 1850 and since then found in several cultivars in gardens and parks. Very wind-resistant, hence used especially in windscreen plantings along the coast. Highly recommended, undemanding wild rose for near-natural gardens. Valuable for small wildlife.

Mountain roses

Mountain rose, pale flowers

Dewberry flowers

Dewberries

Mountain Rose
Rosa pendulina
Rosaceae
Appearance: Loosely branching deciduous wild shrub, 20" to 6½' (0.5–2 m). Leaves stalked, imparipinnate. Flowers borne singly, bright red to pink-purple, lighter at the center, up to 4" (5 cm) across.
Rose hips bottle-shaped, light red or beet-red, edible.
Blooming season: May–July. Fruit ripening in August.
Occurrence: Perennial-herb vegetation and thickets of the European high mountain ranges.

Identification tip: Stems and branches are almost without prickles. Not related to rhododendron genus Alpine rose.
Gardening tip: Suitable as bedding rose for solitary plantings, also in semishade.

Dewberry
Rubus caesius
Rosaceae
Appearance: Deciduous climbing shrub with prickly branches, about 3' (1 m) high. Leaves pinnate, usually with three leaflets. Flowers pure white, in few-flowered umbellike racemes. Fruits are aggregates of drupelets (dewberries), juicy, covered with conspicuous bluish frostlike bloom. Edible, tart-tasting.
Blooming season: May–June. Fruit ripening in August.
Occurrence: Woods edges, thickets, banks, perennial-herb vegetation. Often forms highly impenetrable thickets in streamside and riverside meadows. Widespread in Europe.
Identification tip: The annual branches are round, heavily covered with a greenish frostlike bloom, taking root in the soil again at the tip.
Gardening tip: Recommended for hedge borders.

Blackberries

Thorny branch

Blackberry bush in flower

Blackberry
Rubus fruticosus
Rosaceae

Appearance: Deciduous and partially also semi-evergreen wild shrub, very vigorous, with squared, arching stems up to 6½' (2 m) long. Shoot tips that touch the ground again produce roots. Leaves long-stalked, usually with five leaflets. Leaflets stalked, broad-elliptic, acuminate, rounded at the base, coarsely and irregularly dentate, upper surfaces dull or slightly glossy dark green, undersides light green. Leafstalks and midrib prickly. Flowers pen-tamerous, white or light pink, numerous in terminal panicles on the previous year's branches.
Aggregate fruits (blackberries) juicy, black-red, detach easily from the floral axis. Edible.

Blooming season: June–August. Fruit ripening in July.

Occurrence: Very common along roadsides, on fallow land, along forest borders, in thickets, timber areas, and field hedges.

Identification tip: The common blackberry is a so-called collective species that can be subdivided into several hundred species in North America alone. More precise identification of these small species is very difficult. For practical purposes, assignment to the generic collective name is sufficient here.

Gardening tip: Numerous high-yield cultivars are available for garden use, including some without prickles.

Garden raspberries

Garden Raspberry
Rubus idaeus
Rosaceae

Appearance: Deciduous wild shrub with runners and twiggy, erect (annual) and arching (biennial) stems, 20" to 5' (0.5–1.5 m). Canes round, with a bloom on the surface, and in the lower part covered with black-red prickles. Leaves usually with three leaflets, the terminal pinna being the largest, stalked, upper surfaces hairless, undersides conspicuously covered with white feltlike hair, sharply serrate, rounded at the base.

Flowers white, borne in loose erect or spreading racemes. The sepals are bent back toward the flower. Aggregate fruits (raspberries) consist of numerous drupelets, flesh-red (rarely also yellowish), velvety-haired, easily detachable from the cone-shaped floral axis. Edible.

Blooming season: May–July. Fruit ripening in July.

Occurrence: Widespread in North America and Europe in open woods and thickets, in timber forests, in vegetation of tall perennial herbs, on escarpments and banks, and in rock debris. From the flat-

lands to the mountains.

Identification tip: Even in the nonblooming state this can be easily distinguished from blackberries on the basis of the white-felted leaf undersides and the black-red prickles on the older branches.

Gardening tip: Numerous high-yield cultivars are available for horticultural use; they are derived from crosses with closely related raspberry species from North America. Prefers open, sunny sites.

Bladder senna flowers

Bladder senna fruits (poisonous!)

Scorpion senna in its habitat

Bladder Senna
Colutea arborescens
Papilionaceae
Appearance: Deciduous wild and ornamental shrub, about 3' to 13' (1–4 m). Branches hairy at first, later becoming hairless and hollow. Leaves long-stalked, with five to 11 leaflets, which are short-stalked, broad-elliptic. Flowers borne in racemes having few blossoms, in the leaf axils, golden-yellow. **Fruit and seeds poisonous!**
Blooming season:
May–August. Fruit ripening in July.
Occurrence: Dry slopes, fell fields, open deciduous forests. Primarily in southern Central Europe and in southern Europe.
Identification tip: The pods are parchmentlike and inflated.
Gardening tip: Frequently planted along streets or as ornamental shrub. Highly recommended for edge plantings or solitary use.

Scorpion Senna
Coronilla emerus
Papilionaceae
Appearance: Deciduous wild shrub, 20" to 6½' (0.5–2 m). Leaves long-stalked, with seven to nine leaflets. Flowers borne in umbels having few blossoms, in the leaf axils, pale yellow. Pods long and narrow in structure.
Blooming season:
April–June. Fruit ripening in August.
Occurrence: In open woods and thickets of southern Europe.
Identification tip: The pods are conspicuously narrow.
Gardening tip: Suitable for solitary plantings in sunny, dry places.

Papilionaceae

Lembotropis nigricans

Chamaecytisus purpureus

All parts of *Lembotropis, Chamaecytisus,* and *Cytisus* species are poisonous! In terms of flower biology, they are quite fascinating to observe.

Black Goat's Clover
Lembotropis nigricans
Papilionaceae
Appearance: Thornless deciduous wild shrub, 1' to 3' (0.3–1 m). Leaves thin-stalked, with three leaflets. Flowers golden-yellow, fragrant, borne in large numbers in erect terminal racemes. Pods up to about 1½" (3.5 cm) long, flat. **All the parts are poisonous!**
Blooming season: June–August. Fruit ripening in September.
Occurrence: Open woods, borders of paths and lanes, rocky slopes in sunny posi-

tions. In southern Central Europe and southern Europe.
Identification tip: The leaves, branches, and fruits turn a blackish color in fall or when dried.
Gardening tip: For sunny edges in natural gardens.

Purple Broom
Chamaecytisus purpureus
Papilionaceae
Appearance: Thornless deciduous wild shrub with prostrate stems and ascending branches, 8" to 20" (0.2–0.5 m). Leaves thin-stalked, with three leaflets. Flowers purple-red, borne singly or in

threes in the leaf axils. Pods brownish, slightly sickle-shaped. **All the parts are poisonous!**
Blooming season: May–July. Fruit ripening in September.
Occurrence: Dry thickets, open woods, rocky slopes.
Identification tip: The calyxes are bright brown-red or purple-red.
Gardening tip: For solitary plantings in sunny positions.

Papilionaceae

Chamaecytisus ratisbonensis

Scotch broom in its habitat

Scotch broom, a single flower

Dwarf Broom

Chamaecytisus ratisbonensis
Papilionaceae
Appearance: Thornless deciduous wild shrub with twiggy prostrate or erect stems, up to 20" (0.5 m) high. Leaves long-stalked, with three leaflets, undersides densely covered with appressed hairs.
Flowers yellow-brownish, in lateral clusters. Pods dark brown, densely hairy. **All the plant parts are poisonous!**
Blooming season:
April–June, occasionally once more in September–October.
Occurrence: Woods and thickets, railway embankments and quarries. Central and southeastern Europe.
Identification tip: Inflorescences turning on one side.
Gardening tip: For bed edgings and sunny borders in natural gardens.

Scotch Broom

Cytisus scoparius
Papilionaceae
Appearance: Many-stemmed deciduous wild shrub with squared, green, twiggy branches, about 3' to 6½' (1–2 m). Leaves trifoliolate compound, leaflets ½" (1 cm) long, with appressed hairs.
Flowers golden-yellow, borne singly in the leaf axils. Pods black. **All the parts are poisonous!**
Blooming season: May–July. Fruit ripening in July.
Occurrence: Roadsides, escarpments, forest borders. Acid indicator. Common in western and Central Europe.
Identification tip: When the carina is pressed down, the stamens pop out like a watch spring.
Gardening tip: Very decorative shrub for dry, sunny places.

185

Papilionaceae

Chinese wisteria

Chinese Wisteria
Wisteria sinensis
Papilionaceae
Appearance: Deciduous left-hand twining shrub with thin stems, reaching over 33' (10 m) in height. Leaves long-stalked, imparipinnate, up to 12" (30 cm) long, with seven to 13 leaflets, which are oblong-oval. Flowers appearing before leaves, light blue to blue-violet, very fragrant, in long, hanging racemes. Pods constricted between the seeds. **Poisonous!**
Blooming season: May–June.
Occurrence: Native to East Asia.

Identification tip: The long racemes and pinnate leaves are unmistakable.
Gardening tip: Popular for covering sides of houses. Although it prefers sites exposed to the sun, it also grows satisfactorily in semi-shade. This fast-growing twining shrub cloaks large areas of walls and house sides in a short time. It requires regular cutting back in late fall, because it also penetrates into crevices or joints in the roof covering. The flowers are relished by bees and other hymenopterous insects as a rich source of nectar. If the plant branches very densely, concealing the wall, this species also provides a number of hedge or niche brooders (redstarts) with nesting opportunities. The abundantly produced fruits, which do not always ripen completely, are of minor importance to wildlife, however.

Gorse

Ulex minor

In the western European coastal heaths, the various gorse species bloom almost all year long.
Besides the species shown here, there is also *Ulex gallii* (blooming in late summer or early fall), which is hard to differentiate.

Gorse, Furze, Whin
Ulex europaeus
Papilionaceae
Appearance: Very wide-spreading, densely bushy evergreen wild shrub with erect and spreading branches, 20" to 6½' (0.5–2 m). The dark green branches, marked by lengthwise ridges, are very thickly covered with firm, grooved, sharp spines about 1" (2–3 cm) long, resulting from modification of the foliage leaves. Leaves produced only on seedlings, tri-foliolate compound. Flowers golden-yellow, sweetly scented, up to about 1" (2 cm) across, borne singly or in threes in the axils of long spines or in tiny scalelike leaves along all the stems and branches. Pods up to 1" (2 cm) long, oval, black-brown, covered densely with appressed hairs. **All the parts are poisonous!**
Blooming season: March–July, much earlier in areas with mild winters.
Occurrence: Common to the coastal heath regions of Atlantic Europe from north-ern Spain to the British Isles where it forms groves. On the North Sea islands and in southern Scandinavia, pre-sumably only naturalized.
Identification tip: *Ulex minor*, with unfurrowed spines, grows only to a height of 32" (0.8 m) and blooms in late summer (July–October).
Gardening tip: Frequently planted in meadowland hedges or to separate fields and pastures. The very deco-rative shrub is only barely frost-hardy.

Papilionaceae

All parts of common laburnum are very poisonous!

Common laburnum

Because of its wealth of flowers, laburnum is widely used as an ornamental woody plant. At the same time it is one of the most poisonous deciduous shrubs. Children in particular need to learn early on that these plants are to be enjoyed only with our eyes.

Common Laburnum, Golden Chain, Bean Tree
Laburnum anagyroides
Papilionaceae
Appearance: Deciduous shrub or (multi-trunked) tree with conspicuously smooth bark, about 10' to 20' (3–6 m) high.
Leaves long-stalked, trifoliolate, distinctly alternate on long shoots, clustered in tufts on short shoots. Leaflets up to about 3" (8 cm) long and about 1" (2 cm) wide, oblong-oval, obtuse or rounded at tip, upper surfaces dull dark green, undersides gray-green and with appressed hairs at first.

Flowers light yellow, up to about 1" (2 cm) across, numerous, in hanging racemes reaching 4" to 10" (10–25 cm) in length.
Pods light brown, flattened, and constricted between the individual seeds. **All the parts are very poisonous!**
Blooming season:
May–June. Fruit ripening in August.
Occurrence: As wild shrub, prefers sites on sunny rocks, in open thickets and thin oak stands. From southeastern France through the southern Alps to the Black Sea region.
Identification tip: The

greenish, longitudinally striped bark of the younger stems, the rather large leaves, and the dense, silky, appressed hairs of the shoots and branches are typical. The lower lip of the two-lipped calyx is longer than the upper. In the related Alpine or Scotch laburnum (*Laburnum alpinum*), the lips are equal in size.
Gardening tip: Planted as an ornamental since the sixteenth century. Commercially available in several cultivars that flower more freely than the wild form. Large shrub for background plantings.

Papilionaceae

Alpine laburnum

The golden-yellow papiliona-ceous flowers of the laburnum species are the goal of many flower-visiting insects, princi-pally bees and bumblebees, which can push the wings (alae) and carina aside to take advantage of the offerings of nectar and pollen.

All parts of Alpine laburnum are very poisonous!

Alpine Laburnum, Scotch Laburnum

Laburnum alpinum
Papilionaceae
Appearance: Deciduous wild shrub with erect stems, about 3' to 16½' (1–5 m).
Leaves long-stalked, trifolio-late, in tufts on short shoots. Leaflets oval-elliptic, light green, and slightly glossy. Flowers golden-yellow, fra-grant, very numerous, in hanging racemes up to 16" (40 cm) long.
Pods light brown. **Very poisonous!**
Blooming season: May–July.
Occurrence: On sunny slopes, in open woods and timber forest areas. Moun-tains of southern Europe.
Identification tip: The branches are gray-green and leafless. There exists a fertile hybrid, produced by crossing *L. anagyroides* and *L. alpinum: Laburnum × wateri.* In this form, the leaf under-sides and the flowerstalks are only slightly hairy. Especially conspicuous are the very profusely flowering racemes, up to more than 16" (40 cm) long. The hybrid forms the basis for some decidedly vigorous, very commonly used garden cultivars.

Gardening tip: Like com-mon laburnum, Alpine labur-num and the hybrid are used in parks and gardens as deco-rative background plantings or as components of groups of large shrubs.
Of relatively minor value for wildlife, apart from flower-visiting insects.

189

Winter jasmine leaves

The leaves of winter jasmine are almost opposite at the terminals of the branches. However, farther down, the arrangement is alternate, as in most species of this genus. Because of the very early blooming date, this ornamental shrub is rarely visited by insects.

Winter jasmine in full bloom

Winter Jasmine
Jasminum nudiflorum
Oleaceae
Appearance: Loosely branching deciduous ornamental shrub with slender, very square, arching dark green branches, about 3' to 10' (1–3 m).
Leaves trifoliolate. Leaflets deep green, ciliate. Flowers borne singly in the leaf axils along the previous year's shoots, appearing long before the leaves, light yellow, sometimes slightly reddish on the margins, up to about 1" (3 cm) across, with long, slender corolla tube and five outspread lobes, slightly fragrant.
Blooming season: December–April.
Occurrence: Native to northern China and long cultivated as a showy winter bloomer.
Identification tip: Other species of this genus are in use in parks and gardens.
Common white jasmine (*J. officinale*), native to East Asia, is an erect-growing large shrub that bears large white flowers; it is also cultivated in fields in southern France, primarily for the perfume industry. **Shrub jasmine** (*J. fruticans*) bears yellow flowers and alternate, pinnate evergreen leaves. It is very common in the Mediterranean area and is popular in the warm southern Alps (Ticino, South Tyrol), where it is grown as an ornamental; in some places it grows wild.
Sweet mock orange (*Philadelphus coronarius*) sometimes is also known as jasmine.
Gardening tip: Winter jasmine is of little value for native wildlife.

Hamamelidaceae

Japanese witch hazel

Chinese witch hazel, single flowers

Japanese witch hazel, red-flowered cultivar

Japanese witch hazel foliage

Japanese Witch Hazel
Hamamelis japonica
Hamamelidaceae
Appearance: Deciduous ornamental shrub, about 3' to 10' (1–3 m). Branches spreading, dull gray, covered with stellate hairs.
Leaves broad-oval to rounded, unevenly crenate, short-pointed, with slanting leaf base.
Flowers short-stalked, tetramerous, borne in clusters, golden-yellow.
Blooming season: January–March.
Occurrence: Native to Japan.
Identification tip: The narrow petals always look slightly straggly.
Gardening tip: Japanese witch hazel has been cultivated as a large shrub in Central Europe since the nineteenth century. Of minor value for wildlife.

Chinese Witch Hazel
Hamamelis mollis
Hamamelidaceae
Appearance: Many-stemmed deciduous shrub, 6½' to 16½' (2–5 m) high. Branches densely hairy.
Leaves short-stalked, broad-oval, acuminate, cordate at base and slightly asymmetrical, up to 6" (16 cm) long and nearly 5" (12 cm) wide, both sides hairy, undersides gray-felted. Flowers with wine-red sepals and golden-yellow petals, reddish at base.
Blooming season: January–March.
Occurrence: Native to China.
Identification tip: The narrow petals are not curly, but straight.
Gardening tip: Used in garden culture for many years as an isolated specimen planting. Very decorative, popular species; several cultivars available commercially.

Virginia creeper, fall foliage

Virginia creeper, inflorescence

Boston ivy, fall foliage

Virginia Creeper
Parthenocissus quinquefolia
Vitaceae
Appearance: Deciduous climbing shrub, about 20' to 40' (6–12 m) high. Leaves usually composed of five digitate leaflets, glossy, with crimson color in fall. Flowers insignificant, greenish. Berries pea-sized, blue-black, covered with frostlike bloom. **Mildly poisonous.**
Blooming season: June–July. Fruit ripening in October.
Occurrence: Native to North America. In places, escaped in meadowland.
Identification tip: Leaf tendrils regularly two-rowed, with five to 12 disks. In the very similar **thicket creeper** *(P. inserta),* there are only two to five poorly developed disks.
Gardening tip: Use as for **Boston ivy**.

Boston Ivy
Parthenocissus tricuspidata
Vitaceae
Appearance: Deciduous climbing shrub, up to 33' (10 m) high. Leaves long-stalked, cordate at base, three-lobed at tip (sometimes also unlobed), coarsely dentate, with gorgeous red color in fall. Flowers small, insignificant, greenish, in corymbs. Berries dark blue, covered with frostlike bloom.
Mildly poisonous.
Blooming season: July–August. Fruit ripening in October.
Occurrence: Native to East Asia.
Identification tip: Leaf tendrils opposite the foliage leaves, branched, self-clinging, lacking disks.
Gardening tip: Long cultivated for covering walls and house sides (sunny side). Fruits are eaten by songbirds.

Anacardiaceae

Staghorn sumac in fall foliage

Staghorn sumac, portion of the inflorescence

Staghorn sumac fruits

The name staghorn sumac derives from the fact that the fruit structures bear a remote resemblance to stags' growing antlers (horns), still in their soft, velvety covering.

Staghorn Sumac

Rhus typhina
Anacardiaceae
Appearance: Deciduous shrub with runners or a small tree with erect or outstretched stems, 10' to 16½' (3–5 m) high. Young branches velvet-haired.
Leaves long-stalked, imparipinnate. Leaflets numbering 11 to 31, oblong-lanceolate, coarsely dentate, hairy at first, rich green, undersides light gray, provides splendid red fall color. Flowers small, insignificant, greenish, very numerous, in erect terminal clublike panicles.

Drupes covered with red hair, deep reddish brown or rust-brown.
Blooming season: June–July.
Occurrence: Native to eastern North America. Escapes from cultivation, appears along railway embankments, in places covered with rock debris, or in nutrient-rich, dry herb vegetation.
Identification tip: Smooth sumac *(R. glabra),* also native to Atlantic North America, is very similar. The young branches are hairless and covered with a bluish frostlike bloom; the leaflets are blue-green underneath.

Commonly planted as park shrub or tree, and naturalizes in same places as staghorn sumac.
Gardening tip: Cultivated in Europe as an ornamental woody plant since the seventeenth century. Both sumac species exist in garden forms with deeply pinnatisect or lacerated leaflets. Decorative in appearance, but of no value to wildlife. Undemanding in terms of soil requirements.

193

Identifying Color: Lilac

Shrubs with Needlelike or Scalelike Leaves

The clearly more compact and perennial needlelike leaves are fundamentally different from the usually rather thin-skinned foliage leaves of the deciduous woody plants, with their large surface areas. It is not only the gymnospermous coniferae that have narrow, often very stiff leaves with small surface areas. Other woody plants, classified as angiosperms, simplify their leaf design as well. This modification of the external leaf shape is often the response to a certain environmental factor; it marks a special feat of adaptation.

Common juniper, a light-demanding conifer, prefers open heath areas. Its berrylike cones do not ripen until the second year after the bloom.

Black crowberry flowers

Black crowberries

Black crowberry in its habitat

Black Crowberry
Empetrum nigrum
Empetraceae

Appearance: Evergreen dwarf shrub with prostrate or ascending stems and branches, 4" to 12" (0.1–0.3 m). Forms extensive mats. Leaves very short-stalked, alternate or in small numbers in irregular whorls, leathery, parallel-margined, hairless, glossy dark green. The leaf margins are rolled under and so close together that a narrow groove is created, plugged with a white stripe of hair. Flowers insignificant, unisexual (plant dioecious), greenish-red, with sepals and petals separated, not fusing.

Drupes berrylike, many-seeded, globe-shaped, dull glossy black. Edible, but lacking in aroma.

Blooming season: May–June. Fruit ripening in August.

Occurrence: Primarily in the dunes along the North Sea and the Baltic, in the higher low mountain ranges.

Identification tip: *E. herma-phroditum* is very similar. Its leaves are about ¼" (6 mm) long, and the leaf margins form an acute angle. The flowers are bisexual. The plant's growth habit is more erect; it reaches a height of 20" (0.5 m). Common in the Arctic dwarf shrub tundra and in the Alps.

Gardening tip: Recommended for heath gardens and as ground cover in lime-poor, open sites.

196

Ericaceae

Heather in a north German heath

Heather in flower

Heather, single flowers

Heather

Calluna vulgaris
Ericaceae

Appearance: Many-stemmed evergreen shrub with prostrate and ascending or erect branches, 8" to 20" (0.2–0.5 m). Usually in relatively large stands. Young branches distinctly four-edged. Leaves very small, borne primarily on the short lateral branches, crowded in opposite pairs in four straight rows and overlapping like roof tiles, 1–3 millimeters long and about 1 millimeter wide, stem-clasping at the base, with recurved leaf margins that create a narrow slit between themselves, in summer dark green, in winter bronze to brown-reddish. Flowers tetramerous, hanging, with rose-colored or light violet (rarely also white) petals and markedly longer sepals, very numerous in dense-flowered terminal racemes turning slightly to one side. Capsular fruits inconspicuous, brownish.

Blooming season: July–August. Fruit ripening in September.

Occurrence: On nutrient-poor, acid soils in open pine woods, heath moors, heaths, unfertile meadows, and dunes, as well as on rocky slopes. Widespread in Europe. In the Alps, up to 8529' (2600 m). Also north of the polar circle.

Identification tip: Sole species of the genus and unlikely to be confused with other representatives of the Ericaceae.

Gardening tip: Light-loving, otherwise undemanding species for heath gardens. High-yield source of nectar for flower-visiting insects.

197

Ericaceae

Scotch heath at the edge of cliffs (Brittany)

Fringed heath

Scotch heath, a densely flowered stand

In late summer the cliff regions of Western Europe present extremely colorful spectacles when the various heath species bloom in succession. Scotch heath usually begins the sequence.

Scotch Heath, Twisted Heath, Bell Heather

Erica cinerea
Ericaceae
Appearance: Many-stemmed, loose, dwarf evergreen shrub, 12" to 28" (0.3–0.7 m) high. Young branches squared and gray-felted. Leaves very short-stalked, in whorls of three, linear, with recurved margins.
Flowers tetramerous, brilliant purple-violet, in compact terminal racemes or headlike umbels.
Capsular fruits, inconspicuous.
Blooming season: June–September.

Occurrence: Forms stands in the Atlantic coastal heaths from Portugal to southern Norway.
Identification tip: Leaves are glossy dark green and not sharp-pointed.
Gardening tip: Commercially available in several cultivars as a ground-covering in places with mild winters.

Fringed Heath

Erica ciliaris
Ericaceae
Appearance: Loosely branching evergreen dwarf shrub, 12" to 24" (0.3–0.6 m). Leaves very small, in whorls of three, gray-green, bent down along margin. Flowers bright rose-red, borne in erect terminal racemes up to almost 5" (12 cm) long. Capsular fruits inconspicuous.
Blooming season: July–September.
Occurrence: Singly or in groups in the coastal heaths of Atlantic Europe.
Identification tip: Calyx and corolla long-ciliate.
Gardening tip: Very handsome plant for heath gardens, but not sufficiently hardy in most sections of Central Europe.

Winter heath, inflorescence

Winter heath, single flowers

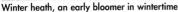

Winter heath, an early bloomer in wintertime

Winter or Snow Heath

Erica herbacea
Ericaceae

Appearance: Many-stemmed, creeping evergreen dwarf shrub, 10" (25 cm) high.

Young branches fairly thin and flexible, hairless, squared and longitudinally furrowed. Leaves in whorls of four, linear, nearly ½" (1 cm) long and less than ⅟₁₆" (1 mm) wide, pointed but not sharp, in summer dark green, in winter more dirty green to brown-red. Flowers flesh-colored to pink, more rarely also pure white, with very short calyx and tubular, short-lobed corolla narrowing at top, slightly nodding, borne in large numbers in terminal racemes turned to one side. Flowers are formed as early as late summer, but maintain dormancy until unfolding.

Blooming season: (December) March–May.

Occurrence: Singly or in stands on rocky slopes or in the border of open coniferous woods in the foothills of the Alps. Usually on limy soils.

Identification tip: The eight dark-purple stamens hang almost completely out of the corolla tube. To dispense pollen, each opens with a lateral split near the tip.

Gardening tip: Also thrives well in lowlands as undemanding ground cover. Commercially available in many cultivars. After the bloom finishes in late spring, the plants need to be cut back by about one third to retain their dense, bushy shape.

Valuable nectar-dispensing plant for insects.

Ericaceae

Crossleaf heath

Cornish heath, white-flowered variety

A valuable aid to identifying the various heath species is the length of the anthers. In crossleaf heath they are shorter than the corolla, while in Cornish heath they are much taller. In any case, they open like a salt-shaker at the top.

Crossleaf Heath
Erica tetralix
Ericaceae
Appearance: Prostrate or erect evergreen dwarf shrub, 8" to 24" (0.2–0.6 m) high. Branches thin and initially thickly covered with matted hair.
Leaves in whorls of four, short-stalked, spreading, linear, usually hairy.
Flowers tetramerous, light pink, in crowded, headlike terminal racemes or umbels.
Blooming season: July–August.
Occurrence: In Atlantic Europe in damp heaths, upland bogs, and acid, damp pine woods. From Portugal to the Baltic.
Identification tip: The calyx and corolla are distinctly ciliate. The corollas turn rust-red after the bloom finishes.
Gardening tip: Not easily cultivated.

Cornish Heath
Erica vagans
Ericaceae
Appearance: Bushy evergreen dwarf shrub, 12" to 32" (0.3–0.8 m).
Leaves in whorls of four or five, linear, ¼" to ½" (5–10 mm) long, dark green, acute.
Flowers with globose corolla, whitish-pink or pale lilac, borne in large numbers in terminal cylindrical racemes.
Blooming season: July–September.
Occurrence: Common along Atlantic coastal heaths of the British Isles, primarily along the western coast of the Channel.
Identification tip: The purple stamens protrude from the corolla.
Gardening tip: Commercially available in several cultivars, but very limited in hardiness.

Tamaricaceae

Tamarisk in flower

Myricaria germanica

Tamarisk in its habitat

Wax Myrtle or Bayberry
Myricaria germanica
Tamaricaceae
Appearance: Evergreen wild shrub with erect, twiggy, brown-red stems, 20" to 6½' (0.5–2 m). Leaves scalelike, sessile, narrow-oval, hairless, bluish green. Flowers pentamerous, white or reddish, short-stalked, less than ½" (8 mm) across, grouped in erect terminal racemes.
Blooming season:
July–August.
Occurrence: Rare, but usually aggressive on gravelly soils on meadows by bodies of moving water. Pyrenees,

Balkans, Scandinavia.
Identification tip: Looks like **heather**. Produces winged seeds with hair tuft.
Gardening tip: Not suitable for garden culture.

Tamarisk
Tamarix gallica
Tamaricaceae
Appearance: Heavily stemmed evergreen shrub or small tree, about 6½' to 13' (2–4 m). Bark purple-brown. Stems and branches twiggy and wide-arching. Leaves scalelike, crowded and spiraling. Flowers pentamerous, pink, short-stalked, borne in

large numbers in dense spiked racemes, and grouped in panicle-shaped entire inflorescence.
Blooming season:
June–August.
Occurrence: Rocky escarpments, coastal dunes, and riverbanks. From northwestern France (Brittany) to the Mediterranean region.
Identification tip: Leaves bluish green. Petals fall after bloom finishes.
Gardening tip: Not hardy in extreme northern United States. Does well from Central New York to Washington State and south.

Tamaricaceae

Hardy tamarisk in flower

Hardy tamarisk inflorescences

Tamarix tetrandra

Hardy Tamarisk, Salt Cedar

Tamarix pentandra
Tamaricaceae
Appearance: Loosely branching evergreen shrub or small tree with twiggy, arching stems, 10' to 16½' (3–5 m) high.
Leaves scalelike, lanceolate-oval, pale green to bluish. Flowers pentamerous, rose-red to dark pink, numerous in spikelike racemes, which are combined in large panicles.
Blooming season: July–September.
Occurrence: Southeastern Europe to Central Asia.

Identification tip: The petals do not fall after the bloom finishes.
Gardening tip: Frequently cultivated as an ornamental shrub since the previous century. Undemanding and hardy.

Mediterranean Tamarisk

Tamarix tetrandra
Tamaricaceae
Appearance: Evergreen shrub or small tree with dark brown to blackish, twiggy, arching branches, 6½' to 10' (2–3 m).
Leaves scalelike, very small, grass-green. Flowers

tetramerous, light pink, very numerous, in clusterlike racemes along the previous year's shoots. Petals fall soon after bloom finishes.
Blooming season: April–May.
Occurrence: Native to southeastern Europe and the Near East.
Identification tip: Unlike the other tamarisks, it blooms in spring.
Gardening tip: More rarely used as ornamental shrub, in some areas used to anchor sandy soils.

English yew with ripe seedcoats

Male flower

Female flower

English Yew, Yew-tree
Taxus baccata
Taxaceae
Appearance: Heavily branching and rather bushy evergreen coniferous woody plant, medium-sized, columnar or broad shrub, 6½' to 16½' (2–5 m), or tree up to 66' (20 m). Leaves up to 1½" (4 cm) long and less than ¼" (3 mm) wide, tapering to a point, upper surfaces glossy dark green, undersides grass-green with two fairly inconspicuous gray-green longitudinal stripes. Along erect shoots leaves arranged in spirals, elsewhere parted in

two rows.
Flowers unisexual (dioecious), borne singly in the leaf axils. Male flowers numerous, globe-shaped, yellowish, with six to eight pollen sacs. Female flowers very inconspicuous, only about 1 millimeter across. Seeds less than ½" (1 cm) long, enclosed in a fleshy, crimson seedcoat covered with a slight frostlike bloom.
All the parts (except the seedcoat) **are very poisonous!**
Blooming season: March–April. Seeds ripening in September–October.
Occurrence: As a wild plant,

usually sporadic in open or shady mixed deciduous woods and ravine woods. From the flatlands to the mountains.
Identification tip: The strong, somewhat flattened needles do not smell aromatic when rubbed between one's fingers.
Gardening tip: Although the wild European form is rarely seen, numerous cultivars are planted in parks and gardens. The black-green columnar yews and the dull green broad, bushy yews are very commonly cultivated.
The seedcoats are a valuable food for birds.

203

Pinaceae

Swiss mountain pine in the Dolomites

Male flowers

Female inflorescence

Swiss mountain pine is a special growth form of mountain pine (*Pinus montana*). In the high mountain ranges, at the climatic limit of the shrubby woody plants, it forms extensive stands of knee timber or elfinwood. Because the weight of the snow presses the shrubs to the ground and they usually grow prostrate, they are also called knee pines.

Swiss Mountain Pine
Pinus mugo
Pinaceae

Appearance: Broad, bushy evergreen coniferous shrub with great diversity of form, usually multi-trunked, with prostrate or ascending stems, about 3' to 13' (1–4 m). Needles in pairs along short shoots, in long, gray-brown needle sheaths, straight or curved toward the shoot in a sickle shape, both sides glossy dark green, finely serrate along the edges. Flowers unisexual: Male flowers yellowish, numerous, in spike-like inflorescences at the base of long shoots; female inflorescences beneath the tip of long shoots, purple-red. Cones very short-stalked, erect at first, later becoming spreading, violet-green when unripe, light brown to medium brown when ripe.

Blooming season: May–June. Cones ripening in the fall of the succeeding year.

Occurrence: Rocky slopes, stony meadows, mountain bogs. In the European high mountain ranges. Up to the alpine region at 7875' (2400 m). Commonly cultivated in North America.

Identification tip: The very short-stalked cones—1" to 2" (2–5 cm) long and equally wide when open—are characteristic. In the high mountains, a variety with an arborescent growth habit known as hooked pine, occurs.

Gardening tip: Planted in numerous cultivars in gardens, parks, and cemeteries as ground covers and dwarf conifers.

Cupressaceae

Common juniper in its habitat

Common juniper, ripe berrylike cones

Common juniper, male flowers

Dwarf juniper in the Alps

Common Juniper

Juniperus communis
Cupressaceae
Appearance: Erect evergreen coniferous shrub with erect columnar or broad bushy growth habit, about 3' to 16½' (1–5 m), rarely also multi-trunked and considerably taller tree. Needles in spreading whorls of three, up to nearly 1" (2 cm) long and less than ¼" (2 mm) wide, very stiff, pointed, and sharp, upper surfaces grooved, gray-green, with wide middle band. Flowers unisexual (dioecious), only in isolated cases also bisexual. Female flowers (cones) with several whorls of scaly leaves, of which the three topmost become fleshy when ripe and coalesce to resemble juicy berries. Berrylike cones very short-stalked, ripening the second year after blooming, red-black, covered with a heavy bluish frostlike bloom. Exudes highly aromatic scent when rubbed between one's fingers. Edible in very small quantities, in larger quantities harmful.

Blooming season: April–June. Cones ripening in July–September.

Occurrence: On nutrient-poor, shallow soils in heaths, unfertile pastureland, semidry lawns, and bordering open woods. Widespread in Europe.

Identification tip: In the Alps and in the dwarf tundra regions of the Arctic, a small, very dense-stemmed creeping form occurs, sometimes considered a separate species: **dwarf or Siberian juniper** (*Juniperus sibirica*).

Gardening tip: Light-demanding woody plant. Mostly used as a solitary plant in numerous cultivars in parks and gardens. The berry-like cones are valuable as food for birds and animals.

Cupressaceae

Savin juniper in its habitat

Male flower

Ripe berrylike cones (poisonous!)

Savin Juniper
Juniperus sabina
Cupressaceae
Appearance: Copiously stemmed evergreen shrub with prostrate, outspread, broomlike stems, about 3' to 6½' (1–2 m), more rarely also gnarled tree with dense, bushy top.
Leaves of different shapes: Young leaves needlelike, arranged in whorls of three. Mature types of leaves scale-like, appressed in intersecting longitudinal rows, obtuse or acuminate, exuding unpleasant odor when rubbed between one's fingers. Flow-ers unisexual, plants monoe-cious or dioecious.
Berrylike cones globular, pea-sized, greenish at first, blue-black when ripe, and covered with heavy bluish frostlike bloom. **Poisonous!**
Blooming season: March–May. Berrylike cones ripening in October of the same year or in spring.
Occurrence: Mostly on limy soils of open rocky slopes, rock debris, in dry meadow-land, open pine stands, and larch forests. European high mountain ranges.
Identification tip: Creeping juniper *(Juniperus horizon-* *talis)*, native to North Amer-ica, exhibits a similar change in leaf shape. Planted in numerous cultivars as dwarf conifers for ground cover.
Gardening tip: Very light-demanding. Used mostly as solitary specimen in open heath gardens. Very drought-tolerant.

Cupressaceae

Red cedar leaves

Chinese juniper fruits (poisonous!)

Besides these two juniper species, the evergreen ornamental woody plants in parks or cemeteries also include numerous other cultivars, some of which are greatly modified. More precise identification of this multitude is quite difficult.

Chinese Juniper
Juniperus chinensis
Cupressaceae
Appearance: Profusely stemmed evergreen shrub with erect or outspread stems, 6½' to 10' (2–3 m) high, or thick-trunked tree with conical top. Leaves vary in design: Young leaves needlelike, in whorls of three, spreading at acute angles, sharp-pointed, upper surfaces with two blue-green longitudinal stripes, undersides dark green. Mature leaves scalelike, arranged in four longitudinal lines, obtuse. Needles and scales exude pleasant,

resinous aroma when rubbed between one's fingers. Flowers unisexual. Male flowers numerous, yellow, borne at the ends of short branches. Female inflorescences insignificant.
Berrylike cones up to about ½" (8 mm) thick, mealy, bluegreen at first, later brownish, covered with heavy bluewhitish frostlike bloom. **Poisonous!**
Blooming season: April–May. Berrylike cones ripening in fall of succeeding year.
Occurrence: Native to Japan, China, and Korea.
Identification tip: In **red**

cedar (*Juniperus virginiana*) also, there appear initially needlelike, later scalelike leaves that are aromatic when crushed. It is native to Atlantic North America, but is rarely planted in the wild form. Very commonly cultivated in a narrow columnar shape.
Gardening tip: Widespread in numerous cultivars as an ornamental woody plant (also dwarf conifers for ground cover).
Insignificant for wildlife.

European thrush in *Crataegus*. Shrub plantings are beneficial for birds and other animals—not only in gardens.

Planting Shrubs

Grainfields stretching across the horizon, sugar beets as far as the eye can see, or acres of level pastures—in many areas, the agricultural landscape looks just that boring and monotonous. No one is likely to fall into a rapture at the sight of such open fields, easy to survey and tailored to accommodate farm machinery. The concept of "field clearing," a popular movement in Germany in the 1960s meant to increase farmland space, was taken literally when these fields were enlarged and made rectangular. Everything that might possibly stand in the way of field consolidation was simply cleared away. Such industrialized agricultural acreage is far removed from the traditional notion of the rural landscape as a source of rest and relaxation, far from an ideal setting for next weekend's hike. There is no visual variety left to experience, because the native plants and wildlife were swept away by the demand for orderliness. Reintroducing shrubs onto cleared fields is a powerful remedy.

Shrubs in the Wild and in Gardens

Rows of shrubbery and meadowland hedges consisting of a variety of species suit the modern cultivated landscape well. In the past few decades, efficiency dictated streamlining much of the green scenic decoration of the rural landscape out of existence. However, what was eliminated urgently needs to be replaced or reestablished, so that the landscape once again is a smoothly functioning network able to perform the tasks so vital to us all.

Meadowland Hedges

Planting a three-dimensionally effective new rural hedge is a project that exceeds the capacities of an individual. But even if you are not the owner or user of relatively large agricultural fields, you still can participate in putting in new shrubs and trees in fields and new hedges along roads and paths. With enough community interest, environmental authorities at the local level may launch planting programs to begin to offset the clear-cutting solutions of the past. Local or regional nature conservation organizations usually are quite willing to take on this task, and hunting associations or forest service offices also translate such measures into action.

Wherever nature conservation groups are active, there is also a fundamental need for helping hands. Because such projects as a rule have to be planned and overseen by professionals, we can disregard here the selection of species and other technical information on the design of a rural hedge.

Woody Plants That Shelter Birds

Scenic beauty and ornament are certainly valid reasons to plant a variety of species in the rural landscape or in gardens, yards, or vacant areas in a community. Another reason—far more important from an ecological standpoint—is the increase in available habitats for small animals that results from planting groups of shrubs or hedges. Anyone who plants appropriate shrub species on a piece of property is simultaneously building a kind of public housing project for threatened wildlife. This is because from its roots to the ends of its branches, a densely growing woody plant has a remarkable system of interlocking small habitats and microhabitats. Scientific research has determined that thickets and hedges in the fields and meadows are among landscape elements with the greatest numbers of animals. A person who plants hedges and shrubs in his or her own garden or who strives to see that these plants are used in appropriate vacant areas in the community creates optimum preconditions for countering the ominous depletion of species on land cultivated by man and influenced by civilization. Birds are often the beneficiaries of such planting. In all seasons, dense boughs are a much-frequented recreation room where birds can rest and relax. Tall central stems are eagerly claimed by song birds, and quite a few species, including the red-backed shrike, use this vantage point as a launching pad for their hunting expeditions into the neighborhood.

In the photo: Splendid backdrop of woody plants. The nitrogen-loving elder is associated with human dwellings or with agriculture. It is a characteristic species of rural settlements in particular.

Woody plants that shelter birds

Planting shrubs

Mockingbirds in a pine, in a mixed stand of shrubs and trees

Wrens, lesser and greater whitethroats, blackcaps, garden warblers, long-tailed tits, serins, greenfinches, linnets, bullfinches, hedge sparrows, nightingales, song thrushes, icterine warblers, and several other birds are pronounced hedge brooders. Their nests are usually so well hidden in the dense maze of stems and branches that we notice them only after the leaves are shed in fall.

In large shrubs or compact thickets one can also attach special nesting aids for hole brooders or semi-hole brooders like redstarts, pied flycatchers, spotted flycatchers, robins, and tree sparrows. These species suffer from a particular shortage of living quarters in the tidied-up agrarian and settled landscape.

The spatial structure alone makes every hedge or bush an ideal bird shelter, offering small birds in particular a host of opportunities. Of course, there is an abundance of things to eat. Many of songbird species are at least intermittently—depending on the available market—highly appreciative fruit-eaters. They consume, without suffering any harm, even fruits that for us are poisonous and dangerous. Forbidden fruits are quite

In the photo: Thickets always extend an invitation for songbirds to harvest, rest, hide, or nest.

different for humans and for animals.

Food for Birds

Even in summer, starlings are beginning to nibble at the first berries of the season. Thrushes dispose of a large part of the wild fruit harvest, and even established insect-eaters like robins and redstarts or whitethroats succumb in late summer to the temptations of ripe elderberries. Biologist Reinhard Witt

Shrubs for animals

once compiled a list of the many bird species that live on certain fruit-bearing wild shrub species. The resulting figures are astonishing. The rowanberry, known in German as the birdberry, does special credit to its German name, as it provides food for more than sixty different species of birds. Redberried elder and juniper feed more than forty species, while cornelian cherry, hedgerow thorn, spindle tree, and European cranberry bush account for at least two dozen.

By no means is the plentiful harvest of the summer and fall weeks always put to use immediately. Even on a walk in late fall or on a sunny winter day it is not uncommon to see wild shrubs still bearing fruit: for example, spindle tree, roses, European cranberry bush, wayfaring tree, hedgerow thorn, and sloe still stand in full array, to speak, even after the true season is past. One would almost think their fruits were vile-tasting, unsalable articles that no beak was willing to touch. In fact, many fruits do contain special flavoring substances that discourage

premature consumption. It takes a few periods of heavy frost to reduce these components. The fruits retained through winter, known as "winter stayers," then provide a very welcome supply just when food is hard to find. These persistent fruits also include the fruits of some ornamental shrubs, such as showy crab apple and firethorn. And what the overwintering birds fail to harvest in their busy roving will be greatly appreciated by the returning migratory birds the following spring. Characteristically, the fruits of some native wild shrubs ripen so late that they are not ready until the first weeks of spring, thus offering stopgap relief at a time when few insects are available. These winter specialists include mistletoe berries and ivy fruits.

Islands of Pollen and Nectar

In addition to songbirds, fruit-eating small mammals such as hedgehogs, dormice, lerots, muscardins, bank voles, squirrels, and the like benefit in different ways from shrubs. For insects, too, our native shrubs are distinctly inviting. In early spring, quite some time before the leaves are produced, some species open their flowers and hold ready a high-grade supply of pollen and nectar.

Shrub willows and cornelian cherry are among the very early nectar-supplying plants, not only for bees, but for bumblebees and butterflies as well. Because in some areas, the gardens occupy areas larger than nature preserves and wilderness areas combined, you can imagine how important

In the photo: In autumn, the hedge fruits are the major items in the birds' diet.
A starling in a spindle tree.

213

Planting shrubs

Swallowtail butterfly caterpillar

White C

Polydamus swallowtail butterfly

Viceroy

Swallowtail butterfly

In the photos: All the developmental stages, from egg-laying to the completed butterfly, require woody plants as habitat structures.

near-natural gardens, equipped with a wide variety of plants, are for protection of the species as well. Apart from the annual summer flowers and free-flowering herbaceous plants, it is the shrubs that have a special role in that effort. Shrub species with especially slender-tubed corollas are extremely popular with butterflies (both diurnal lepidoptera and moths). Butterfly bush, also known as summer lilac, is exceedingly attractive—one of the few examples of an imported ornamental woody plant that has special value for small wildlife. Not only diurnal butterflies, like painted ladies, peacock butterflies, and red admirals, visit the lovely inflorescences—it is also worthwhile to take a close look some evening or night and marvel at the bustling activity of the numerous butterflies that are active at twilight or after dark. Along with summer lilac, the Caprifoliaceae, as well as aromatic plants like thyme, sage, and lavender, are particularly productive sources of nectar for butterflies.

Don't forget that quite a few shrubs also provide the food that caterpillars require—alder buckthorn for the brimstone butterfly, birch and field elm for the mourning cloak butterfly, honeysuckle for the viceroy, goat willow for the purple emperor, sloe and hedgerow thorn for the swallowtail butterfly.

Shrubs As a Focal Point—in Villages and Cities Too

Trees and shrubs in the rural landscape—except for wooded areas and cultivated forests—are either scattered as single plants or combined in rows or groups, and in this way they give special emphasis to the characteristic terrain features of the countryside. In settled areas as well, they have an important aesthetic role to play.

Basically, the spatial functions of stands of woody plants in a rural community are equivalent to the functions of large trees within a city. In both cases the plants, by virtue of their size alone, act as parts of a stage set, catching the eye and forming a backdrop. The commercial and residential buildings of a village look far more appealing if they are flanked by single trees, rows of shrubs, or small groups of shrubs and trees. In the city too, the unending lines of gray, cube-shaped masses of stone

Shrubs in villages and cities

and the monotony of continuous rows of facades can be visually interrupted if a number of relatively large woody plants stand next to the solid structures. The general appearance of settled areas, whatever their size, can be more effectively enhanced by shrubs and trees than by any other means.

In rural areas, woody plants near a village have an additional role of tying the entire locale into the countryside. In the city, groups of shrubs and trees can make a more attractive transition from the built-up area of human habitation to the regions surrounding the city, which are defined by a completely different type of land use.

Even industrial facilities look less severe when they are surrounded by tall, broad-leaved shrubs and trees and if they are not completely exposed on an otherwise bare plot of ground.

Green instead of Gray

What is true for the uniform ensembles of solid structures also applies to individual buildings. The immediate surroundings of public buildings can be made more appealing with the right selection of ornamental woody plants. Using shrubs and trees in this way beautifies administration buildings, hospitals, churches, and schools. In an agreeable way, they also lessen the obtrusiveness of many structures that have huge proportions.

Private residential and commercial buildings too appear more attractive when they display a few cosmetic touches—woody plants near buildings and in yards and gardens. Trees and shrubs break the stony sameness of our daily lives.

A final, especially important point to consider is that, it is not only a matter of applying green cosmetics and making our resi-dential landscape fit for a picture book, but of creating an acceptable environment as well. With every additional shrub that is allowed to grow, flower, and bear fruit in our family's ornamental or vegetable garden, we create a small, but essential, counterbalance to offset the loss of many areas that we have developed. Woody plants are almost always the right means for adding visual variety and making our surroundings pleasant—provided you use species that are appropriate to the site and the landscape.

For various reasons, many home and garden owners, when planting shrubs and trees—particularly in neighborhoods of new homes—tend to show a disproportionate preference for coniferous species alien to their region. More than a few yards turn out

Planting shrubs

badly, becoming demonstration areas for the attractively priced assortment of conifers at the nearest garden center. Instead of a hedge of arborvitae or a uniform row of Omorika pines, indigenous broad-leaved species would be a worthy alternative. Numerous handsome wild shrub species can also be found to serve as ecologically valuable replacements for azaleas, rhododendrons, smoke tree, corkscrew hazel, and quite a few other trendy shrubs and trees.

Shrubs for the Garden

Apart from their varied uses and irreplaceable ecological value, hedge shrubs are also a highly practical accessory for house and garden or for farmstead and countryside.

Previously, one of the major tasks of hedges and shrubbery was to define the limits of plots of land and to safeguard them. In many regions, including Brittany, England, Wales, and the lowlands of northern Germany it is the custom even today to surround pasturelands or sections of farmland with hedgerows, in order to divide the areas of activity of cattle, horses, or sheep into parts small enough to be seen at a glance and easily supervised, or in order to keep the grazing animals out of certain sections.

A dense hedge is a highly reliable safeguard. A thick growth of shrubs or small trees that is kept sufficiently dense and compact through appropriate maintenance procedures fully replaces a fence made of netting wire or barbed wire, and without a doubt it looks much more attractive than a solution using stone or metal.

For Security, Use a Hedge

The same is true also for a hedge in a settled area. A sufficiently dense medium-sized or tall hedge, equipped with attractive thornbushes, is an obstacle that is both insurmountable and impenetrable. It keeps unwanted visitors at a distance and also denies stray dogs a congenial gap to slip through. By contrast, it does provide a welcome invitation for songbirds such as thrushes, whitethroats, and hedge sparrows. As in the well-planted rural landscape, hedges in built-up areas permit only local border traffic involving hedge-dwellers or small animals like stone martens or hedgehogs. In addition, a hedge meets the need for a privacy screen facing the street and/or the neighboring properties. And last but not least, a living fence is more appealing and natural than fortifications like concrete walls or wire entanglements.

In the photo: There are suitable shrub species for many kinds of biotypes, even for the edges of bodies of water.

Shrubs for the garden

Hydrangeas next to a Breton farmhouse

Everything speaks in favor of using hedges, not only in the open countryside, but also in the realm of home and garden. The changing picture throughout the seasons, ranging from leaf production through flowering to the decorative fruits of the late summer and fall weeks, overcompenates for the few chores needed to maintain a hedge around your house or yard so that it can perform its many ecological and technical functions over the long run. And in comparison to tending a bed of flowers or vegetables, taking care of a hedge is not time-consuming.

In the photo: Garden hydrangeas display the full beauty of their flowers only in areas with mild winters.

Shrubs Near the House

Woody plants are important and effective components of a healthy environment. There is always enough room for a few special shrubs or trees as accents, even in very tiny areas near the house or in the yard. Once all the legal issues have been investigated, and locally applicable minimum distances have been ascertained, you can begin to plan and choose among several possible designs. You can either design a beautifully tiered backdrop of woody plants of various heights that still preserves a certain openness, or you can create a more tightly closed hedge planting that stresses boundaries and surrounds your yard with a high green wall. In either case, form goes hand-in-hand with the intended function. Mixed solutions somewhere between solitary plantings, dense groups of bushes, and tall hedges are also realizable. If circumstances permit, even a combination that includes green climbing plants on the side of the house has a charming effect.

Green Façades

Forbidding, bare house facades and bleak, unattractive expanses of wall are often all too common in our modern landscape. But where unimaginative architecture has simply set down unshapely, faceless masses of stone and concrete in the landscape without regard for aesthetics, all is not lost: The vivid beauty of green plants is always a remedy.

A Concealing Disguise

Fast-growing twining and climbing plants can disguise the harsh lines of many a structure with appealing shades of green and thus provide an endurable visual tie-in to the surroundings. Moreover, they offer so many distinct advantages with respect to the microclimate and to radiation, wind, and pollutants, one really wonders why great skepticism is still so widespread and why this simple and effective use of green plants is not more common. In addition, many taller-growing climbers need amazingly little room for their roots, so that they seem quite appropriate even for city houses with little space between them. A green— or multicolored, depending on the season—mantle of plants not only looks appealing, but may perhaps create a few much-needed and effective suggestions of closeness to nature, even in the midst of urban desolation. Then why not let a pleasing backdrop of greenery grow right on the ugly boundary wall or the boring building façade?

Second-story Artists

The various *Parthenocissus* species, which can be put to a great variety of uses, are able to manage without artificial climbing supports. With or without adhesive discs, depending on the species, they can easily make their way up even completely perpendicular surfaces. They are deciduous and make their final bow in fall with a spectacular display of color.

If you prefer an evergreen cloak, use English ivy. However, its adhesive aerial rootlets force their way into crevices and joints as they seek to anchor themselves, and after decades they can seriously erode and loosen the spots where they cling.

Other twining and climbing shrubs that are also well suited for covering very tall houses or steep walls are grapevine, which promises a rich yield of fruit particularly on walls with plenty of sun, and Chinese wisteria, which delights us with its early summer flowers borne in great profusion.

Where covering house sides with greenery from basement to gable is less important than making a wall several yards high

Greenery-covered houses

The courage to take cover: a facade cloaked in Virginia creeper

look somewhat more attractive, traveler's joy, other *Clematis* species, climbing hydrangea, and the twining honeysuckle species are advantageous. Finally, dog rose also softens the contrast between an abruptly looming wall and the rest of the surroundings. The last-named shrub species may be very grateful for climbing supports such as lattice panels, wire netting, or hooks doweled into the wall.

Designing Groups
The species used to landscape your home naturally have to be chosen on the basis of the shape, size, and orientation of the lot. Once you have decided on one or two trees for your landscape which I unreservedly recommend for visual and space-enhancing reasons, you can start selecting the shrubby plants. In this case, you should place a few large shrubs in solitary plantings or in small groups beside these trees, which are eye-catching in any event, in order to interlace the plants in a more interesting, spatially effective way. It makes sense to arrange these specimens, which after a few years can reach quite a respectable girth as well as a backdrop-

In the photo: Greenery on the side of a house is not only an outstanding ecological achievement, but advantageous from a landscape architecture standpoint as well.

forming mature height, at the back of the yard (preferably on the northwest to northeast sides). Enough room will be left in the foreground to accommodate free-flowering herbaceous plants or summer flowers.
Large shrubs recommended for a visually very effec-

Planting shrubs

tive and simultaneously decorative border or background planting would include, for example, serviceberry, red dogwood, common laburnum, European elder, hedge maple, sloe, or one of the two *Crataegus* species.

Where the space allows, you can plant a loose group of handsome wild shrubs to create very appealing tiered solutions that in appearance closely approximate the graduated arrangement of the woody plants at the edges of woods or thickets. Because many native shrubs naturally occur in woodland undergrowth and hence are thoroughly shade-tolerant, you can use the same method to landscape the areas without sun exposure on the north and northeast sides of a house or to fill in other corners created by buildings, where sun-hungry summer flowers grow poorly anyway.

For those portions of the lot which are somewhat darker all year round, these shrubs are well suited: privet, common spindle tree, alder buckthorn, holly, and hornbeam, which normally has a treelike growth habit.

House and Garden Hedges

Although hedges in the open countryside and in settled areas perform a number of very similar tasks, there are also certain differences that you need to keep in mind when choosing the right plants for a hedge.

Hedges in fields and meadows are intended to create links, and they often have a great deal more room in which to develop into units of woody plants. However, on more modestly sized residential lots they are likelier to produce a thick green border enclosing your property or to serve as a privacy screen, warding off curious gazes. For these reasons, they have to be kept in shape by regular pruning.

Cutting Back to Increase Density

A classic box-shaped hedge of privet, which has to be sheared at least once a year to preserve its shape, is certainly a greater gain for the immediate residential environment than gloomy, dark green walls of yew or arborvitae, which tend to lend to the yard the charm of a cemetery. Far more attractive and a great deal more effective for species conservation in your own yard is a wild hedge with as much diversity as possible. It will supply variety all year long, because the various hedge shrubs will bear flowers and fruits at different times.

If you force the hedge into a highly rigid geometric box shape by intensive pruning, you will suppress the development of the flowers and fruit to a certain extent. Wherever it is feasible, you should give a house or garden hedge a certain amount of space for development, so that it has a chance to display its seasonally changing adornments.

Picture-pretty Hedges

Of the deciduous shrub species, the following tolerate pruning especially well and are recommended for a hedge including a mixture of various species and defining a property boundary: privet, barberry, hedgerow thorn, sloe, dog rose, wayfaring tree, and European fly honeysuckle.

Legal Problems at the Property Line

If there is no love lost between two neighbors, it may be the fault of the garden shrubbery. Like everything else in life, the utilization and landscaping of your own property can become an issue, or even a court case. Conflicting rights of usufruct and tax evaluations become all the more explosive the closer

In the photos: Special bark structures such as corky ridges, spines, or lenticels perform special tasks or serve as species characteristics.

Bark types

Spindle tree

Basket willow

European cranberry bush

Blackberry

Dewberry

Tatarian dogwood

Lichens

Planting shrubs

Colorful variety at the boundary of the yard

you get to the boundaries of the yard.

In cases of doubt, nature conservation organizations can provide additional assistance in the form of useful suggestions. Provisions are usually rather general where the law of neighbors is concerned.

Local Border Traffic

Falling leaves that trickle onto the property next door or are blown by the autumn wind into the neighborhood are not a legal issue, then. The flight of seeds from wild plants that colonize a near-natural garden in certain numbers, according to recent interpretations of the law, is also not deemed an unlawful defilement of the natural environment, but a normal manifestation of life on the part of the tree or shrub, and it has to be accepted as such. The most important restrictions affirmed by the law of neighbors of the German Länder have to do with the bound-

In the photo: Mixed hedges of various deciduous shrubs, arranged according to height, are extremely decorative. They also expand the range of habitats available in the yard.

ary distances that must be maintained by plantings of shrubs and trees.

With very large-growing tree species, which lead us to expect an expansive and correspondingly shade-producing development of

Legal problems at the property boundary

the treetop, the planting distance from the property line has to be at least 13' (4 m). With smaller trees and large shrubs, a distance of at least 6½' (2 m) has to be observed between the planting hole and the boundary. Low hedge plants up to a mature height of about 6½' (2 m) have to be set at a distance of 20" to about 3' (0.5–1 m). Apart from these minimum distances, you can plant trees and shrubs on your property as you like.

For rather small lot sizes, an ecologically valuable planting of shrubs and trees can become very difficult to achieve while observing the prescribed minimum distances to the exact inch. In such cases, it is useful to reach agreements on any divergent details of the boundary planting separately, with the appropriate neighbors.

In the photo: Spectacularly abundant flowers along with amazing growth. Wisterias require climbing supports.

Planting Shrubs

Many native shrub species are ecological specialists. Some species, such as Scotch gale or marsh tea, prefer wet, boggy soils, while others, like mahaleb cherry or cotoneaster, favor dry, rocky sites. Some very decorative shrubs, such as scorpion senna and bladder senna, are at home in warm climates; others, like black crowberry or Scotch heath, prefer the damp Atlantic climate with its mild winters. Usually it is impossible to provide the appropriate preferred conditions in your own yard for shrubs with such special needs and predilections.

Soil Requirements

Luckily, most shrub species are not overly fussy in respect to soil quality. Many indigenous wild shrubs are species from woodlands or from edges of woods, and the shrubby plants of the open fields and meadows also grow on what once were wooded sites. Because garden soils for the most part are derived from average farmland, or can be treated—with a few exceptions—shrubs like the conditions near houses and in yards and gardens.

Preparing the Soil

Where a tract of land has been used for gardening

Preparing the planting pit: At the site, dig down at least two spade-lengths deep, remove the soil, then thoroughly loosen an additional spade-length.

for a fairly long time, special preparation of the soil before planting shrubs is generally unnecessary. However, planting them in a newly developed area is a different matter. Here the soil is often extremely compacted, or the topsoil has been carted away by the truckload during the excavation of the foundation pits. For most garden shrubs and trees, you can create acceptable start-up conditions by loosening the soil thoroughly, by digging down at least twice the depth of your spade, and by improving the soil with materials such as green manure, sawdust, chaff, shredder products, compost, or bark chips (not peat!).

After setting the plant stock, water it copiously. Make sure each plant is set at the right depth in the loosened soil!

Finally, fill the planting pit with topsoil or compost humus, making sure to leave watering space all around, about 4" deep. The top of the roots (where the small trunk begins) should be just barely above the surface of the soil. Regular watering after planting improves the shrub's ability to strike root.

Suitable species

Soil Care

Once the planting has become well established, subsequent soil care can be restricted to occasional, careful loosening of the surface. Regular applications of commercial fertilizers are not required.

To ensure that enough plant nutrients are available, I recommend using a much better material, one that in addition conforms to the natural conditions in the shrubs' wild habitat: In summer, from time to time, you can spread grass clippings under the shrubs and let them decay there on the ground. In fall, after you have raked leaves, put some beneath the shrubs, or apply some of the shredded waste obtained when your herbaceous beds were cleared away.

Choosing the Species

Creating an alpine garden full of small woody plants from the high mountains when you live in a lowland area is just as absurd as planting an Atlantic heath garden at the higher altitudes of the low mountain ranges. In choosing shrub species for use in your landscape, you should be guided as much as possible by the environment and the site. A walk through local woods or fields will give you a good idea of what is typical for a certain area and what belongs in the inventory of woody plants for your garden.

Exotic plants are certainly very rewarding in their own particular homelands. In the wrong spot or in a completely alien environment they usually are of little ecological value, however.

Plant Stock—Bought or Home-grown?

No real nature lover will go out to the nearest stand of woody species in the fields or the closest wooded area with a folding spade and simply make off with the plant stock needed for his or her own garden, even if the shrub species in question are neither rare nor even specially protected. There are other, far less problematic ways to acquire a rich variety of species for your home landscaping project:

<u>Start Them Yourself</u>

You can unhesitatingly bring back a very few(!) seeds or fruits from a vacation trip, a weekend outing, or an afternoon walk, with the idea in mind of growing your own plants. Seeds from pomes and drupes or berries, as well as nuts (hazelnuts, beechnuts, acorns, chestnuts) should be planted in normal garden soil in a flowerpot of adequate size. Then dig a hole for the pot in a vacant bed and bury it in the ground. After the seedlings of the woody plants germinate and grow stronger, plant each one in its final destination in the garden.

Seeds from dry fruits (capsules and pods) can be stored dry over the winter. In spring, start them in the standard way, in seed-starting containers or shallow pots. If they become too crowded, transplant them and thin them out. Once they reach a height of about 6" to 12" (15–30 cm), you can set them out.

<u>Cuttings</u>

Many deciduous woody plants can be propagated relatively easily by cuttings. Candidates for this type of propagation include box, privet, European elder, sea buckthorn, viburnums, willows, and cotoneasters. For this purpose, use terminal branches about as long as your hand, taking them from strong annual stems. Take the cuttings preferably after the leaves fall but before the first frosty nights. Over the winter, heel them down in damp sand, with the ends protruding about one finger length. Cover them with fallen leaves, sawdust, chopped straw, or bark mulch. In the spring, simply stick them outdoors in garden soil or in large seed-starting containers, leaving enough room between them, until they are ready for planting the following season.

Planting shrubs

Spindle tree

Tatarian dogwood

Smoke tree

Forsythia

Evergreen beech

226

Buying Plants

The easiest method of obtaining the right plant stock in the proper sizes and amounts is to pay a visit to a garden center or a nursery. Sometimes it is also worthwhile to ask at the nearest forestry office (if there is one nearby). All wild shrubs are available as nursery plants, but all the species you want may not be on hand at all times.

Planting Shrubs

The best planting date for so-called balled-and-bur-lapped stock is October. Seedlings or juvenile plants that are rooted in the large pot in which they were grown from the start (container-grown plants) can be planted at any time during the growing season, from March to November. It is important to dig a large enough planting hole and also to loosen the soil in its vicinity, so that the roots can develop well. Regular watering in adequate amounts is essential, especially while the plant is striking root.

In the photos: The enormous wealth of leaf shapes is enhanced in fall by special color accents. Here, a selection of particularly brilliant fall colors.

How Many Plants?

When you plant a normal, bushy wild hedge you need three to four shrubs per running yard (1 m) for a single-rowed planting and twice that number for a double-rowed planting.

For a box-shaped hedge, you should calculate five to six plants per yard (1 m). Working out a planting plan for the selected shrub species in advance will help you determine the right amount of stock to buy.

Care of Shrubs

In extremely wind-exposed places—for example, at the top of the coastal cliffs in the Atlantic east—regular maintenance of shrubs is totally unnecessary. Here the constant wind stress, which has the same effect as steadily clicking pruning shears, ensures that tops and branches become denser.

Farther inland, garden shrubs and hedgerows almost always need upkeep.

Pruning Is Important!

Pruning is the most important type of care for woody plants. This procedure allots the various shrub species the room they need for growth, keeps fast-growing species somewhat in check, and promotes those less able to compete. For most woody plants, the best time for maintenance pruning is the period of

Wild shrubs at a glance

	for dry soil	for moist soil	needs lots of light	tolerates semishade	also flourishes in shade	suitable for hedges	tolerates pruning	especially lovely flowers	decorative fruits	important for small animals
Alder buckthorn		•		•	•	•		•		•
Barberry	•		•	•		•	•	•	•	•
Blackberry	•	•	•	•		•	•	•	•	•
Buckthorn	•		•	•		•	•	•		•
Crataegus laevigata		•	•	•		•	•	•	•	•
European cranberry bush		•	•	•		•	•	•	•	•
European elder		•	•	•		•	•	•	•	•
European hazel		•	•	•		•	•	•		•
Goat willow		•	•	•		•	•	•	•	•
Hedge maple	•		•	•		•	•			•
Hedgerow thorn	•		•	•		•	•	•	•	•
Holly	•	•	•	•	•			•		•
Juniper	•		•					•		•
Privet		•	•			•	•	•	•	•
Raspberry	•		•			•		•		•
Red-berried elder		•	•	•		•	•	•	•	•
Red currant	•			•				•		•
Red dogwood	•		•	•		•	•	•	•	•
Sea buckthorn	•		•					•		•
Serviceberry	•		•			•	•	•	•	•
Sloe	•		•	•		•	•	•	•	•
Spindle tree		•	•	•		•	•	•		•
Wayfaring tree	•		•	•		•	•	•	•	•
Wild roses	•		•			•		•	•	•

dormancy between the end of October and the beginning of March (see table). The cutting should be done on frost-free days, with strong and above all sharp hedge clippers, pruning shears, or lopping shears. Make the cuts as close as possible to the trunk or main stem. Each cut ming or shaping: It stimulates the production of new shoots and branching. It involves removing the largest and farthest-spreading branches about every four years, cutting them back to where they join the stem on the old wood or back to the ground, while still preserving the overall few of them each year over a period of several years, always leaving enough growth for wildlife to take shelter in.

Consider Groups at the Edges

Wherever groups or rows of shrubby plants grow at woods edges or in the rural

Pruning Dates for Woody Plants

	Jan.	Feb.	Mar.	Apr.	May	Jun.	Jul.	Aug.	Sep.	Oct.	Nov.	Dec.
Berry bushes	•									•	•	•
Deciduous formal hedges							•	•	•			
Evergreen hedges			•	•								
Fruit trees	•	•									•	•
Other shrubs	•	•									•	•
Roses			•	•						•	•	•

should slope vertically. If the cut surfaces are larger than a quarter, apply tree balm (available in garden stores) to protect against fungal infections and rot.
• Thinning removes overly numerous small trunks and stems from woody plants grown in parks and gardens. With hedges in the open countryside, which are meant to reach a certain density, this type of pruning is unnecessary.
• Cutting back has an effect much like that of the far more common trim- appearance of the shrub or group of shrubs.
• Drastic or renewal pruning removes the majority of the trunks and stems of a shrub to about 8" to 12" (20–30 cm) above the ground. With field hedges in particular, this method should be employed every 15 to 20 years, to prevent them from developing into a row of trees and to renew the vigor of the shrubs.
With relatively large hedgerows, however, never reduce all the stems to the stock. Selectively cut a landscape, they often are surrounded by a fringe of wild herb vegetation. The same look can be achieved in a shrub-filled garden where the emphasis is on a near-natural appearance. The area beneath or in front of the individual shrubs is by no means off limits for additional planting and landscaping. For example, it is well suited for numerous spring bloomers that undergo their entire development from sprouting to bearing fruit at about the time the

Undergrowth and edge plantings

Mountain rose in various stages of flowering

woody plants are producing leaves. Besides snowdrops, crocus, yellow star of Bethlehem, and harebells, you can use other plants to great advantage here: daffodils, Christmas flowers, wood anemones, liverwort, wood primrose, celandine, creeping bugle, and March violets. Also suitable for enhancing the edges of rows of shrubs are species that appear in the agricultural landscape in so-called edge or border communities. Along with white dead nettle, spotted dead nettle, and yellow archangel, the following would be likely candidates: stitchwort, ground

ivy, greater celandine, and lampflowers. Sweet woodruff also spreads out nicely beneath stands of shrubs. Very shady places next to or beneath shrub groups in a garden can also be planted with native wild ferns, and the results are both decorative and ecologically valuable. In addition, large-growing species such as common male fern and woodland lady fern or somewhat smaller species like polypody and beech fern can be used. They, as well as the equally suitable hart's-tongue fern, are sold as container-grown stock in garden centers.

In the photo: Only single-flowered roses are of value to our native fauna.

Poisonous Wild and Ornamental Shrubs

Even the shiny black fruits of deadly nightshade look somehow tempting and inviting. However, nature's glossy offerings, should not always find their way into the kitchen, because many plants are, after all, extremely—in some cases even fatally—poisonous. Such species need not be

Planting shrubs

rigorously banned from your garden, however; rather, you just need to know how to deal with the problem. It is especially important to know the species in question with looks at all colorful and juicy. The dangers presented by wild and ornamental shrubs are basically no greater than for other decorative garden plants such as foxglove (digitalis) garden in which small children will spend time.

Shrub Species (selection)	Poisonousness			Poisonous Plant Parts	
	poisonous!	dangerous!	caution!	shoot/leaf	seed/fruit
Alder buckthorn		•		•	•
Boxthorn	•				•
Broom species	•		•	•	
Buckthorn	•				•
Cherry laurel	•			•	•
Chinese wisteria	•				•
Daphne			•	•	•
Holly	•				•
Honeysuckle	•				•
Ivy	•				•
Laburnum			•	•	•
Privet	•				•
Red-berried elder	•				•
Savin juniper		•		•	•
Scotch broom	•				•
Snowberry	•				•
Spindle tree		•		•	•
Viburnum species	•			•	
Yew		•			•

certainty. Because it is primarily the ripe(ning) fruits that present the greater danger, as opposed to the leaves and flowers, even small children have to be taught that under no circumstances are they to swallow everything that and scarlet runner (French bean).

The problem of poisoning can be effectively forestalled with precautionary comments, and if that is not possible, simply do without the poisonous species when planting a

In the photos: A great many wild and ornamental shrubs bear poisonous fruits in fall—here, a selection.

Poisonous fruits of wild and ornamental shrubs

English ivy

Common yew

Alder buckthorn

European fly honeysuckle

Privet

Mahonia

Wayfaring tree

Virginia creeper

European cranberry bush

Red dogwood

Spindle tree

Snowberry

February daphne

Cherry laurel

Holly

For reference

Index

The page numbers in **boldface** type refer to photographs.

Index

Index

Index

Index

Index

English translation © Copyright 1995 by Barron's Educational Series, Inc.
Published originally under the title *Sträucher in Natur und Garten* by Grafe und unzer Verlag, GmbH, Munich, West Germany
Translated from the German by Kathleen Luft.

Library of Congress Catalog Card No. 94-46431

International Standard Book No. 0-8120-9203-1

Library of Congress Cataloging-in-Publication Data

Kremer, Bruno P.
[Sträucher in Natur und Garten. English]
Shrubs in the wild and in gardens / Bruno P. Kremer.
    p.   cm. — (Barron's nature guide)
Includes index.
ISBN 0-8120-9203-1
1. Shrubs—Europe. 2. Ornamental shrubs—Europe. 3. Shrubs—Europe—Identification. 4. Ornamental shrubs—Europe—Identification. 5. Shrubs—Europe—Pictorial works. 6. Ornamental shrubs—Europe—Pictorial works. I. Title. II. Series.
QK281.K7413   1995
635.9'76—dc20   94-46431
                                              CIP

Printed in Hong Kong
5678   9955   0987654321

European elder (see page 171)

Garden raspberry (see page 182)

Many wild shrubs bear edible seeds and fruits in fall—here, only a small selection drawn from nature's bounty.

Wild apple (see page 145)

Blackberry (see page 181)

Rock currant (see page 141)